FAST BIKES
THE NEW GENERATION

FAST BIKES
THE NEW GENERATION

Colin Schiller

First published in 1987 by Osprey Publishing Limited
27A Floral Street, London WC2E 9DP
Member company of the George Philip Group
Reprinted spring 1988

British Library Cataloguing in Publication Data

Schiller, Colin
  Fast bikes.
  1. Motorcycles, Racing
  I. Title
  629.2'275   TL440
ISBN 0-85045-761-0

Editor Tony Thacker
Design Roger Walker

Filmset by Tameside Filmsetting Limited,
Ashton-under-Lyne, Lancashire
Printed in Hong Kong

Page 1 **Suzuki's RG500 Gamma, the best of the short-lived breed of two-stroke 500 cc Grand Prix replicas**

Pages 2–3 **The class of '84: Yamaha's 138 mph two-stroke RD500LC takes on Honda's 125 mph four-stroke VF500**

Right **Ducati tried their hand at fully-enclosed bodywork with the highly original Paso 750**

Below **Bimota's DB1 redefined motorcycle aesthetics with its stunning execution of Ducati's V-twin 750**

Contents

About the author

Colin Schiller is a leading motoring writer and photographer contributing to many motorcycle and car magazines both in the UK and abroad. From 1984–85 he was editor and chief road tester of *Which Bike?* magazine, and has exhaustively ridden and tested almost every new superbike from Italy, Germany and Japan since 1982. Here he traces the development of each new sports bike since 1984, including first-hand road impressions and independent performance figures for each machine, and provides the most definitive catalogue of performance bike tests so far available in book form. Combined with superb action photographs, *Fast Bikes* is a unique portrait of the world's most prestigious performance bikes over the last three years.

Acknowledgements

Every author has a whole list of people to thank because producing a book is definitely *not* a one-man effort. So thanks to Richard Francis for his pictures of the Kawasaki GPx750 and Don Morley for his shots of the Honda CB1000. Thanks, too, to *Bike* magazine who kindly allowed me to reproduce many photographs which first appeared in that publication.

Finally, I owe my gratitude to a very special breed of rider who gets a buzz out of performing for the camera: Mike Heath, Chris Dabbs, Mick Gooden, Roland Brown and Mac McDiarmid.

Colin Schiller
London, England
March 1987

Foreword

You don't need to be an international road racer to appreciate the amazing development in road bikes over the last 20 years. Back in 1967 when I was starting my racing career, motorcycles were still in the dark ages: noisy, smelly, dirty and thoroughly socially unacceptable. True 100 mph performance was still a fantasy, handling was more often than not like an airport trolley, and stopping quickly meant having massive great soles on the bottom of your boots. In those days, even indicators seemed futuristic!

The influence of race-bike design both in the 1970s and, more importantly, the early 1980s, revolutionized motorcycle engineering so completely that by 1983 1100 cc road bikes were pushing out 120 bhp with the potential to top 150 mph. Even that seemed tame, however, by the standards set in 1985–86 when road-bike construction didn't simply ape race-bike design, it paralleled it. Both Yamaha and Suzuki turned out 500 cc replicas of mine and Kenny Roberts' Championship-winning GP two-strokes that were so impressive that in modified form they proved more than competitive at national racing level and could easily best 150 mph.

Even more impressive than that, however, was the continuing development of four-strokes whose power output trebled from the sedate 45 bhp Bonneville of 1968 to the staggering 135 bhp now turned out by the 1987 Yamaha FZ1000R, some 15 bhp more than my own 1976 World Championship-winning 500 cc two-stroke. At 170 mph, top speeds too are not far off those being achieved by Grand Prix machines.

Moreover, chassis, suspension and brake design has now become so advanced that lap records set by pukka race bikes in the 1983 Isle of Man TT were being bettered last year by standard road bikes. I only wish they'd built them like that when I was serving my apprenticeship!

Fast Bikes is a fascinating catalogue of the best in that development since 1983, properly road tested by Colin Schiller himself (who knows a lot more about road bikes than I do) and superbly photographed by him too in his own inimitable style. If you want to know about modern superbikes, *Fast Bikes* is the most authoritative directory currently available.

Barry Sheene
Surrey, England
March 1987

Left **Chris Dabbs shows how the professional rides for the camera**

Right **Barry Sheene on the 1981 JPS Yamaha taking Kork Ballington for a pillion!**

Introduction

I well remember the time I saw my first superbike; cruising along the North Circular in London on my ageing BSA C15 250, having signed my life away to some grubby insurance pirate in N22, I caught the glimpse of a vision in turquoise and chrome, singing its way northwards. As a devotee of British bikes, ignorant of motorcycle sport and the new technology it was spawning, I was mesmerized. My previous impressions of Japanese sports bikes had conformed to the parochial anglophile cliché of plastic-looking, electric-sounding, high-revving two-strokes, high on performance but low on machismo. What I saw was the antithesis of all that. It looked *huge*, I mean colossal; four massive cylinders sprawled out underneath an enormous, glaring, aquatic-blue petrol tank; mile upon mile of exotically-crafted chrome emanated from the front of an exactly sculptured mill; the seat looked like a sofa by Meriden's standards, and the rear tyre had the widest section I had ever seen. It burbled ruggedly on the overrun and literally sang on the open throttle. It was a dream. It was a Honda CB750K0.

That one motorcycle, regardless of what Kawasaki achieved with their legendary 900 in the following year, revolutionized the entire world bike industry by combining previously-undreamt-of levels of performance with a pattern of reliability that British bike builders had considered unachievable. Far from being a glitch-ridden prototype, the sohc, air-cooled transverse four sustained a remarkable record of service, despite its 70 bhp (later detuned in the K1 to 65 bhp) which propelled it to a genuine 125 mph (some say nearer 130 mph). Its combination of performance, reliability and looks, not realized in previous Japanese sports bikes, converted a generation of British-bike bores into consumer junkies, unable to resist the innovations from the land of the rising sun. In one form or another, the Honda survived until 1978.

Even then, only a handful of later models could have outpaced it.

Although Kawasaki responded within a year to the precocious 750 with their own faster, and more sophisticated, dohc 900, the true second generation of Japanese superbikes followed almost a decade later with Honda's outrageous six-cylinder, 24-valve 1000 cc CBX. It is true that Suzuki could be proud of their achievement in the GS1000, which was probably the best combination of handling and performance available in the late 1970s, but Honda's CBX, which handled appallingly, provided the experience in engineering compactness that led to nimbler, multi-valve superbikes in 1979.

After a decade of unbridled lust for more power, the Japanese finally got the message that 600 lb of cast alloy did not seem quite so accomplished on bumpy English B-roads as it did on Californian highways, and the next four years in Japanese superbike design saw engineering progress concentrated on the chassis. By 1984, 120 bhp 16-valve engines, capable of nudging 150 mph and scorching through the quarter-mile in well under 12 seconds, propelled 600 lb all-up weights which were cradled in alloy box-section frames, damped by rising-rate suspension and stopped by twin-pot opposed-piston disc brakes. Who could possibly want or need anything more?

The Third Generation

Japanese analysis of the European market concluded that what we both wanted and *needed* was more replica race-bike engineering. Specialization was their answer to the stagnation of Western sales. At the end of 1983, three bikes were announced that would shatter previous conceptions of superbike performance for the third time. Ironically, for the first time, none of these was a Honda; two were Yamahas (the RD500LC and the FJ1100) and one a Kawasaki (the GPz900R). Now nudging 160 mph, ten-second quarters, and weighing 20 per cent less than their predecessors, they moved motorcycle design into a new era. At the time of writing, 1987 looks set to be the culmination of that third generation.

Left **The white elephant of 1985. Kawasaki's GPz750R, overtaken by the sheer pace of development, proved to be just a slower Ninja**

Yamaha RD500LC

It was the bike that journalists had been dreaming of and dreaming up ever since Yamaha introduced its legendary RD350YPVS two-stroke. In 1983, several magazines had run spoof road tests on what they imagined a full-size, GP race replica 500 two-stroke would look and perform like. Perhaps, in the end, this is what convinced the factory to produce it. Certainly, no one could have been disappointed, for the new 500, with 87 bhp on tap, ran a genuine top speed of 140 mph, a whisker over 12 seconds through the quarter-mile, and handled quite unlike any other mass-produced machine previously available. It also looked stunning.

In fact, the RD owed less to Kenny Roberts' 1983 Grand Prix machine than it did to the simple RD250 production bike; similarities with the racer began and ended with it possessing four cylinders in a (50-degree) V-configuration and incorporating a power valve. The 500 was really two 250s with their separate, contra-rotating crankshafts joined together by a central jackshaft. Barrels were separate castings for each pot, and while the rear two cylinders used reed valves, case reeds were adopted for the front two. To preserve the space between the cylinders for the four 26 mm power-jet carburettors, the exhausts ran fore and aft, the

back pots being reversed for rearward exit. The 56.4 × 50 mm bore-and-stroke engine was liquid-cooled and lubricated by an automatic oil pump.

Similarly, the frame, a box-section fabrication, diverged from works GP practice in that it was made from steel, rather than alloy, and conformed to full-cradle tradition, rather than using the engine as a stressed member à la racer. Low centre of gravity was aided by making the top rails run wide around the engine, rather than over it, and siting the rear rising-rate monoshock horizontally beneath the mill (basically, because there was nowhere else to put it). Front forks were conventional oil-damped telescopics with anti-dive, and the brakes were of the superb opposed-piston variety acting on ventilated discs.

If the RD set new standards for 500 cc performance, it also established new parameters for handling. At 390 lb, and with the most precise front end ever designed for a production motor-cycle, it was compared to pukka racing tackle by every tester who rode it. The bike could be hurled into corners harder and deeper than anything else, courtesy of the V4 engine configuration, the front wheel staying firmly planted on the tarmac even at severe angles of lean. The suspension, though marginally soft at the rear, was excellent overall, and the bike's handling was such that a good rider could have beaten almost any other bike under 1000 cc on any 50-mile cross-country dash.

The combination of superb, almost unparalleled stopping power and exhilarating, but not too peaky, two-stroke delivery allowed Michael Dowson to take a production 500 to race victory at its début in the prestigious Castrol six-hour endurance series in Australia, beating a dozen four-strokes of twice its capacity. No tester achieved less than 135 mph on the bike, and one magazine claimed 148 mph, though 140 mph seems to have been its true top road speed. A shorter first gear would have dropped quarter-mile times to less than 12 seconds. The overall impression of riding the 500 fast was of homogeneity, continuity and balance, rare enough in a four-stroke, let alone a two-stroke 500 works Grand Prix replica.

Faults? The 500 had only a few. Poor finish and detail design plus engine vibration from the jackshaft were the most obvious, apart from the fact that, despite everything the 500 had going for it, the bike did not sell particularly well. In the main, this was due to the fact that the market for which it was intended simply could not afford the £3000 price tag.

Yamaha RD500LC

Engine:	Reed-valve two-stroke V4
Capacity:	499 cc
Bore × stroke:	56.4 × 50 mm
Compression ratio:	6.6:1
Carburation:	Four 26 mm Mikuni
Power:	90 ps @ 8500 rpm
Torque:	49.9 ft/lb @ 8500 rpm
Chassis:	Box-section steel double-cradle frame with alloy swing arm
Front suspension:	Telescopic fork with four-position anti-dive
Rear suspension:	Monocross with preload and damping adjustment
Front brake:	Twin ventilated discs with opposed pistons
Rear brake:	Single ventilated disc with opposed pistons
Tyres:	Michelin A/M48: 120/80V16 front, 130/80V18 rear
Wheelbase:	1375 mm (54.1 in.)
Rake/trail:	64 degrees/95 mm
Weight:	178 kg (392 lb) dry
Fuel tank:	5.93 gallons
Top speed:	138 mph
Standard quarter:	12.52 sec
Fuel consumption:	34 mpg
Range:	200 miles

Laverda Corsa

While the Japanese paused towards the end of the first generation of superbikes in 1977, a small Italian factory, whose previous engineering expertise had been based on the design and production of combine harvesters, stood poised to wrest the performance laurels back from the Far East. The factory of Laverda had developed its established 3CE 1000 to an awesome combination of rugged power and reliability that, for a year at least, was to prove unbeatable. This bike was the 1978 Jota, the only production bike able to run a *genuine* 140 mph *and* handle as well. No suprise, then, that it wrapped up that year's Avon production championship by a huge margin.

Laverda's limited development capital, however, and the inexorable progress of the high-tech, high-capital Japanese factories meant that by 1980 the Japanese were parading the performance crown once again. Then, as if their historical timing could not have been better, when the second generation of Japanese superbikes lost their impetus momentarily in 1983, Laverda's new and most radical bike, the 1000 cc Corsa, was ready to carve itself a sizeable share of the big-bike market once more.

The Corsa was Piero Laverda's expression of where he thought big-bike development should be heading in the second half of the 1980s, with the emphasis on its dual roles as a sports bike and a tourer (almost the opposite of the Japanese theory of model specialization). Previously, the 1978–81 Jota and the 1982 Jota 120 had provided few concessions to comfort or civility, and Laverda's dwindling share of the market with this bike was mistakenly interpreted by the manufacturers as a thumbs-down to unequivocal sports bikes. Thus, the Corsa was the heart of the revised 120-degree-crankshaft Jota, polished and ported for even more performance, but draped in the luxury touring clothes of the company's other new bike, the

innovative RGS. Its novelty, like the RGS, was the tank-filler mounted high in the fairing, but the bike's real significance was as the culmination of everything that was good about Laverda's four-stroke engineering and chassis design.

Unlike the 1978 Jota, this Laverda really handled, due in large part to the new double-cradle chassis which reduced the overall elevation of mass and lowered the riding position. Most of the chassis' constituent parts were remarkably traditional, but because the initial geometry was spot on, the bike steered as sweetly as anything Japan could offer. It also held the road tenaciously and, with £600 worth of fully-floating Brembo Goldline racing calipers, stopped very dramatically.

The 981 cc, dohc three-cylinder engine was purely an upgrade of the 1982 120, the crankshaft (as the earlier bike's name implies) being

Laverda Corsa

Engine:	Dohc transverse triple	Rear brake:	Single 280 mm fully-floating Brembo Goldline
Capacity:	981 cc		
Bore × stroke:	75 × 74 mm	Tyres:	Pirelli Phantom 100/90V18 front, 120/90V18 rear
Compression ratio:	10.5:1		
Carburation:	Three 32 mm Dell'Orto	Wheelbase:	1500 mm
Power:	85 bhp @ 6000 rpm	Take/trail:	Not available
Torque:	Not available	Weight:	540 lb including 1 gallon of fuel
Chassis:	Duplex cradle	Fuel tank:	4.8 gallons
Front suspension:	40 mm Marzocchi forks	Top speed:	145 mph (estimated)
Rear suspension:	Two Marzocchi Strada with five-way preload adjustment	Standard quarter:	11.8 sec (estimated)
		Fuel consumption:	35 mpg
Front brake:	Twin 280 mm fully-floating Brembo Goldlines	Range:	170 miles

designed so that the cylinder fired at even intervals rather than the 180's two-up-one-down arrangement. This made the engine a lot smoother and altered the torque curve so that the legendary peakiness of the 1970s bike was banished for good. In addition, the Corsa's compression ratio was raised, and all ports and inlet tracts were hand-fettled and flowed. Bigger exhaust diameters and improved breathing produced an overall figure of around 90 bhp, which was moderate by Japanese standards but quite adequate to propel the aerodynamic shape of the Corsa's fibreglass to around 145 mph. Certainly, it was the fastest production bike Italy had ever produced.

Moreover, unlike almost any other Italian motorcycle, the Corsa was smooth, civilized and comfortable. Three years earlier, these adjectives would not have been admissable in the same paragraph as the legendary Laverda name.

Unfortunately, history was against the Corsa, for it was only on sale (at £4750) for about eight months before Yamaha launched its similarly-marketed FJ1100. The latter was not only a genuine 150 mph-plus machine, but was also a superb tourer.

Yamaha FJ1100

Where the accomplished nature of the RD500LC was only to be expected as the culmination of Yamaha's unquestioned supremacy in building high-performance two-strokes, the accomplishment of their FJ1100 in turning the big-bike sports/tourer market on its head was something of a surprise, for Yamaha, of all the Japanese factories, had the patchiest of records in building high-performance four-strokes.

As an unabashed copy of some of the established Bimota principles, the FJ changed all that in an instant. Its 1098 cc, air-cooled transverse four, with four valves per cylinder and the alternator carried behind the cylinder block, rather than riding on the end of the crankshaft, followed established Yamaha principles. But the overall compactness of the engine and its colossal 125 bhp, housed in what Yamaha referred to,

somewhat pretentiously, as a 'lateral concept frame', provided a combination of performance, reliability and handling that, until December 1984 and the launch of Kawasaki's GPz900R, could not be bettered.

In fact, the lateral concept frame referred to on the bike's fairing was simply a box-section steel fabrication with its top two rails joined in front of the headstock to give it greater lateral rigidity. The more innovative part of the chassis was its peripheral nature, i.e. the way the same two rails braced the engine from its sides rather than running over the top of it. Geometrically, this provided a lower centre of mass. It also reduced both seat height and the overall frontal aspect, improving the bike's drag coefficient and aiding performance significantly.

Not surprisingly, with the inclusion of several of the essential Bimota ingredients (i.e. 16 in. front and rear wheels, a huge 150-section rear tyre, and the overall similarity of the chassis), the FJ1100 steered faultlessly at all speeds and, for its engine displacement, was remarkably nimble. The, by now, standard Yamaha monocross, rising-rate rear suspension, coupled with massive 41 mm front stanchions with anti-dive, gave a progressive, if slightly soft, ride for an out-and-out sports bike. However, by the time Kawasaki had announced and previewed its GPz900R, Yamaha was at pains to point out that the 1100 had always been intended as a sports/tourer. Even though this seems unlikely, the shrewdness of the twist in emphasis was a marketing masterstroke, and the FJ seemed to find its own niche with the slightly older, more

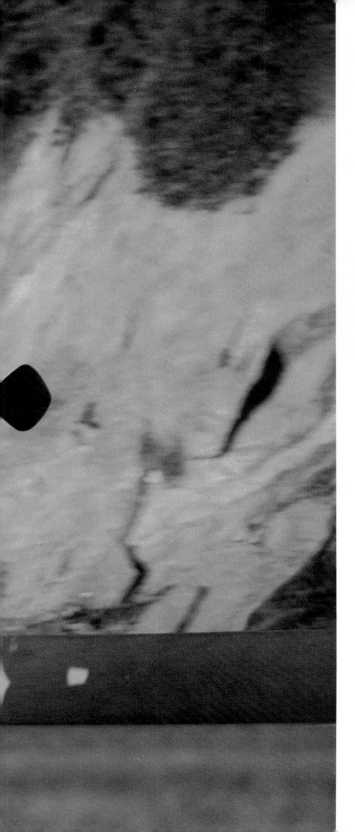

mature rider that kept it separate from the more adolescent RD350 graduates who, undoubtedly, would plump for the sportier Kawasaki.

The simple, rugged, air-cooled engine was ideally suited to the dual sports and touring roles. It could push through the standing quarter in a shade over 11 seconds, yet tow a tractor in top gear at 3000 rpm. Its top speed of 150 mph plus (some claimed nearer 155 mph) was almost academic— above all, it was the ease with which it got there, and for this reason, the summer of 1984 saw the roads of Europe crammed with more British-registered FJ1100s than any other big road bike. Comfort, on such a compactly executed bike, was as excellent for 6 ft 4 in. hulks as it was for 5 ft 4 in.

road racers. Perhaps the FJ's only significant fault, as a top-line corporate flagship, was its poor record on corrosion.

By December 1985, with the advent of the FZ750's new four-stroke technology, the FJ's touring role was consummated by boring it out to 1200 cc and augmenting its long-distance features. Its virtues are still particularly apposite today, and it remains the standard by which others are judged in the sports/touring category.

Yamaha FJ1100

Engine:	Dohc 16-valve four-stroke four	Front brake:	Twin opposed-piston calipers with 280 mm discs
Capacity:	1097 cc		
Bore × stroke:	74 × 63.8 mm	Rear brake:	Single opposed-piston caliper with 280 mm disc
Compression ratio:	9.5:1		
Carburation:	Four 36 mm Mikuni	Tyres:	Dunlop 120/80V16 front, 150/80V16 rear
Power:	125 bhp @ 9000 rpm		
Torque:	75.9 ft/lb @ 8000 rpm	Wheelbase:	1490 mm
Chassis:	Full-cradle 'lateral' box-section perimeter frame	Rake/trail:	62.5 degrees/4.4 in.
		Weight:	556 lb (dry)
Front suspension:	41 mm fork with three-way adjustable damping and preload and four-way adjustable anti-dive	Fuel tank:	5.4 gallons
		Top speed:	152 mph
		Standard quarter:	11.33 sec @ 118.29 mph
Rear suspension:	Alloy swing arm with monocross suspension adjustable for preload and damping	Fuel consumption:	43.5 mpg
		Range:	225 miles

Kawasaki GPz750 Turbo/ Harris 750 Turbo

In a list of the top 20 bikes of the last five years, the GPz750 Turbo might be hard to justify. However, its significance as the most eloquent orator of its short-lived and short-favoured species is undeniable.

Unfortunately, the principles of turbocharging, so effective and efficient on the average modern aluminium car engine, do not fit easily on the back of the significantly smaller-capacity motorcycle mill. Where the simple addition of a bolt-on blower might add 50 per cent extra power to a car without any compromise or alteration in handling characteristics, the extra power generated from a

motorcycle engine may not be worth the sacrifice in agility. In fact, Kawasaki were the last of the four Japanese factories to try the compressed-air performance formula and may well have learned from the compromises and mistakes made by Honda, Suzuki and Yamaha. All three companies' attempts at turbocharging produced motorcycles with handling that was either quirky or unsatisfactory in the sports category for which their engines were intended.

Kawasaki's approach was much more straightforward: they took a well-handling bike with an excellent power-to-weight ratio and added the

turbo in a position that gave maximum power for minimum cost. They found this to be right underneath the exhaust headers, which reduced lag to a minimum and kept the unit's extra weight as near to the ground as possible. The consequent transformation of their standard GPz750's sedate 80 bhp into the electrifying 112 bhp of the Turbo makes you wonder why the other Japanese factories did not follow the same path. Kawasaki's legendary engineering overkill also meant that few of the engine's original constituent parts had to be altered significantly to deal with the extra 30 per cent of power generated by the blower; a new plate for the clutch here, a stronger bearing for the output side of the gearbox there. Apart from digital fuel injection instead of carburettors and the necessary

Left **The 'unblowered' GPz900 proved faster and far more manageable than the 'cult' 750 Turbo**

lower-compression pistons and revised cam timing, it was the old GPz750 that the world knew and loved.

The power the bike was making, when the turbo cut in, meant acceleration like a 250 two-stroke race bike. Top speed was conservatively estimated at 135 mph, and the standing quarter-mile was equally impressive, at just over 11.2 seconds. Suspension revisions, plus shorter, stiffer forks and a heavily-braced frame, may have helped deal with all the extra power, but they could not disguise the fact that the 750 now tipped the scales at an ungainly 550 lb. Not surprisingly, even though the Kawasaki was in a different league to the poor-handling Honda CX650 Turbo and Suzuki XN650 Turbo, it could no longer cut it with the performance class of 1984, which included the same company's GPz900R launched at almost the same time. To be honest, steering was ponderous, and the combination of high all-up weight and quirky Michelin

A/M48 tyres—plus the inevitable lag present in all turbos—produced handling that was sometimes quite worrying.

Aware of the potential in this impressive power-plant, Ricky Hunt, special builder extraordinaire and owner of a crashed 750 Turbo, built what had to be the most impressive turbo motorcycle yet produced. In late 1984, he managed to shoehorn the Kawasaki power-plant into a Harris Formula 1 chassis with the minimum of modifications to both engine and frame. Ricky's engineering skill and design brilliance produced a bike some 150 lb lighter than the factory's, with acceleration and performance figures that were not bettered until a whole year later by the Japanese themselves. Acceleration was phenomenal, with 150 mph achievable in less than half a mile. With the correct gearing, the Ricky Hunt 750 Turbo could have run at 160 mph. Ricky had proved, too late, that turbos could work on motorcycles.

Kawasaki 750 Turbo/Harris Kawasaki Turbo

Engine:	Dohc turbocharged four-stroke four	Dohc turbocharged four-stroke four	Front brake:	Twin 280 mm discs	Twin opposed-piston Lockheed calipers with anti-dive
Capacity:	738 cc	738 cc			
Bore × stroke:	66 × 54 mm	66 × 54 mm			
Compression ratio:	7.8:1	7.8:1	Rear brake:	Single 270 mm disc	Lockheed floating caliper with 260 mm Brembo disc
Carburation:	Digital fuel injection	Digital fuel injection			
Power:	112 ps @ 9000 rpm	112 ps @ 9000 rpm	Tyres:	Michelin A/M48: 100/90V18 front, 130/80V18 rear	Michelin TG22: 120/80V16 front, 160/60V18 rear
Torque:	73 ft/lb @ 6500 rpm	73 ft/lb @ 6500 rpm			
Chassis:	Duplex tubular cradle frame	Duplex tubular cradle frame	Wheelbase:	1490 mm	1435 mm
Front suspension:	40 mm fork adjustable for damping and preload with four-position anti-dive	42 mm fork with damping adjustment	Rake/trail:	63.5 degrees/ 4.12 in.	64 degrees/ 4.25 in.
			Weight:	515 lb	392 lb
			Fuel tank:	3.75 gallons	5.4 gallons
			Top speed:	135 mph	155–160 mph (estimated)
			Standard quarter:	11.3 sec @ 117 mph	10.8 sec @ 128 mph
Rear suspension:	Uni-Trak monoshock adjustable for damping and preload	White Power monoshock adjustable for damping and preload	Fuel consumption:	42 mpg	45 mpg
			Range:	155 miles	240 miles

Honda VF1000R

With the exception of the VF750F (the top-selling 750 in 1983), the lack-lustre performance of Honda in its traditional area of market domination, the big-bike arena, had led the company to develop an arsenal of weapons ready for the summer of 1984. It seemed natural to them that a bored-out development of their 750 cc class leader would be quite enough to scupper the supposedly con-servative and traditional transverse fours from Kawasaki and Yamaha. Thus, the mass-market VF1000F was launched in early 1984 as more than a match for its class rivals. However, in case Honda had underestimated the opposition, they also kept up their sleeve the VF1000R, a limited-edition production machine which, although £1500 more expensive than the opposition's top-of-the-range

model, would nevertheless prove that Honda, if they really wanted, could still build the biggest, the best, the fastest.

At least, that was the theory, and there was no doubt that the gear-driven dohc V4 engine could run with the best of them. However, despite its impressive 125 bhp and superb traction, the VF1000R failed to outrun either the incredible GPz900R or the supposedly more leisurely FJ1100. Indeed, it was only 6 mph faster than its cheaper (by £1700) brother which, at 149 mph, was also outpaced by both the Yamaha and Kawasaki. The real surprise was that its handling was not impressive either, largely because no matter what Honda added in the way of trick suspension and box-section framework, they just did not seem to be able to make the V4 engine configuration manageable in a production road bike.

Of course, Joey Dunlop was having incredible success on the race version of the bike, which made the reluctance of road-test reviewers seem even more irrelevant. But, when rising Grand Prix star Wayne Gardner let slip in a press interview that a VF1000R he had ridden in the prestigious Castrol six-hour race in Australia handled appallingly, the doubts of mere mortal reviewers seemed fully justified. After all, his was a bog-standard production bike; Joey Dunlop's was a race-built one-off special.

With a 524 lb bike, however, perhaps Honda were being a little optimistic that they could stifle the generally slinkier opposition. Despite the 16 in. front wheel, response to the handlebars was slow and cumbersome, and in tight turns, the bike felt almost top-heavy. In a straight line, it was incredibly stable and impressive; in turns, it was anything but.

It was not all bad, however. Launched a year earlier, the 1000R might have been unassailable. But time waits for no motorcycle manufacturer, and

the relentless march of progress in design meant that Honda's traditional policy of building the biggest was no longer appropriate. Other features, such as the styling, the fairing and some of the detail and finish work, put the machine in the true superbike class, but it seemed that the people who could afford the £5250 price tag opted for a Bimota instead. After all, why buy mass-produced exotica when you could afford hand-built exotica?

The truth is that the 1000R left Honda with egg on their faces in more ways than one. They had painted themselves into a corner from which they could not escape by insisting that the V4 principle was the correct one and that Honda would remain committed to it. Despite this, only one more V4 four-stroke was to emanate from the Honda factory. By early 1986, Honda had announced the impending launch of its new range of sports bikes. All were— surprise, surprise—in-line fours.

Honda's VF1000F sold disappointingly and handled only marginally better

Honda VF1000R

Engine:	Dohc 16-valve liquid-cooled 90-degree V4	*Front brake:*	Twin dual-opposed-piston calipers with 275 mm discs
Capacity:	998 cc	*Rear brake:*	Single dual-opposed-piston caliper with 215 mm ventilated disc
Bore × stroke:	77 × 53.6 mm	*Tyres:*	120/80V16 front, 140/80V17 rear (radial)
Compression ratio:	11:1		
Carburation:	Four 36 mm Keihin CV	*Wheelbase:*	1505 mm
Power:	122 ps @ 10,500 rpm	*Rake/trail:*	62 degrees/3.9 in.
Torque:	67.8 ft/lb @ 8000 rpm	*Weight:*	524 lb (dry)
Chassis:	Box-section steel duplex cradle frame	*Fuel tank:*	5.5 gallons
Front suspension:	Air-assisted 41 mm forks with anti-dive and adjustable rebound	*Top speed:*	155 mph
		Standard quarter:	11.19 sec
Rear suspension:	Alloy swing arm with Pro-Link monoshock adjustable for rebound damping	*Fuel consumption:*	35 mpg
		Range:	190 miles

Bimota SB4

Whatever aspirations of exclusivity the VF1000R may have had, one aspect of the Bimota it could never live up to was cost—£8000 at 1984 prices. Bimotas had always been expensive, but in 1984 they became truly outrageous, with the inevitable consequence that the UK concessionaires sold only three or four bikes, countrywide, that year.

This was something of a tragedy, for the SB4 (S = Suzuki, B = Bimota, 4 = fourth in that particular series) was by far the finest motorcycle the Rimini factory had produced to date. Even with the technologically-dated Suzuki GSX1100 engine, the SB4 could still push 150 mph and provided a standard of handling which no other motorcycle could live up to.

The secret of the SB4's magic was, as on all Bimotas, the perfect geometry of the frame and the brilliance of its integration with available suspension systems. Such was the perfection of the chassis that Bimota felt able to eschew the now-fashionable, box-section fabrication. Instead, they crafted the SB4's bones from simple chrome-moly tubing. TIG-welded at every joint and augmented by aircraft-specification, straight-cut alloy plates at the intersection of frame and swinging-arm rear suspension and engine mount, the SB4 trellis provided the inspiration for Yamaha's FJ1100

If not the fastest, at £8250 (1984 prices) the SB4/HB3 easily proved the most exclusive

Left **The Bimota SB4 could be ridden right down to the lettering on its tyres**

Above **Honda-engined HB3 was the only guise in which the 16-valve 1100 motor appeared in UK**

lateral concept. It consisted of a lower full cradle and top rails that ran wide round the engine, hugging the latter from both sides, and joined in front of the headstock for greater rigidity. All it weighed was 33 lb.

Suspension components, such as 41 mm Ceriani racing forks replete with Goldline fully-floating, opposed-piston calipers and rising-rate rear De Carbon monoshock (a first for Bimota) with variable preload and damping adjustment, were the best in the business. But it was their integration with the chassis and not their individual technical specification that was so impressive. Unlike the new breed of Japanese sports bikes with 16 in. front wheels, the Bimota, which pioneered small

front wheels, felt like it had been born with the wheel, not merely had it tacked on. The SB4 provided a perfect lesson in steering design, combining agility with absolute neutrality and precision. Similarly, the suspension, though uncompromising to comfort, performed with the control and progression necessary for a sports bike. Directional stability was perfect, and both low-speed and high-speed cornering took road-bike handling into a new era. On the Bimota, you could enter a corner 10 mph faster than on any other bike, lose the line completely, and still come out 20 mph faster than anything else. Chassis flex was kept to a minimum, suspension movement was hardly discernible, and the progressive power

of the Brembo Goldlines was something of a revelation compared to the brute force and grabbiness of most similarly-equipped Japanese sports bikes.

The Bimota exuded quality in every respect, from the specification of the metals through to the design and finish of every component, including their own yokes, bars, footrests and fairing. The GSX1100 motor provided the SB4 with a somewhat harsh and vibratory feel, but without airbox and with Bimota's own-design exhaust pipes, the 115 bhp available was enough to keep the 450 lb SB4 in the same performance league as the latest Japanese bikes which had an extra year's advance in technology and development. If the Bimota had a fault, it was probably the rawness of its drive-train and the almost complete absence of working instrumentation—details the Italians never seem to worry about. But there is a price for paradise, and anyone who had ridden an SB4 would have been more than prepared to pay it.

State-of-the-art fully-floating Brembo Goldline disc brakes accounted for £600 (1984 prices) of the Bimota's £8000-plus price tag

Bimota SB4/HB3

Engine:	Suzuki or Honda. Specification here refers to Suzuki dohc 16-valve four-stroke four	*Front brake:*	Twin 280 mm opposed-piston Goldline Brembos
Capacity:	1075 cc	*Rear brake:*	Single 280 mm Brembo Goldline
Bore × stroke:	72 × 66 mm	*Tyres:*	Michelin A/M48: 12/80V16 front, 150/80V16 rear
Compression ratio:	9.5:1		
Carburation:	Four 34 mm Mikuni CV	*Wheelbase:*	1435 mm
Power:	111 bhp @ 8500 rpm	*Rake/trail:*	Not available
Torque:	70.9 ft/lb @ 6500 rpm	*Weight:*	466 lb (dry)
Chassis:	Chrome-moly tubular steel space-frame with lower cradle	*Fuel tank:*	4.8 gallons
		Top speed:	146 mph
Front suspension:	Ceriani 40 mm forks and seven-position rebound adjustment	*Standard quarter:*	11.74 sec
		Fuel consumption:	55 mpg
Rear suspension:	Box-section swing arm with rising-rate De Carbon shock adjustable for preload and damping	*Range:*	250 miles

BMW K100RS

Almost at the same time that the Japanese were entering a qualitatively new era of development, the lone European volume manufacturer, BMW, was also set to revolutionize its product line. Hitherto, the company had depended on the simple, elegant, very effective, horizontally-opposed twin design to maintain its share of the market against very sophisticated competition. Although the 'Boxer' had performed incredibly well, BMW realized that they could not rely on such an agricultural design to carry them into the latter part of the twentieth century, whatever its utilitarian virtues. Their dilemma lay in how to replace a machine their philosophy and advertising copy had repeatedly claimed was the only true motorcycle engineering solution. Furthermore, they had effectively burned their bridges by insisting that the

The BMW K100—longitudinally-mounted, water-cooled and injection-managed

Japanese approach was not only unnecessarily complicated and a whim of fashion, but inherently wrong. How, then, could they enter the twenty-first century without performing a giant U-turn and avoiding confronting the Japanese head-on for the same slice of the market?

Their answer, somewhat paradoxically, was to employ a car designer on the new bike who came up with the 'compact-drive' system, which is now the basis of the entire BMW range. This consisted of a water-cooled, in-line (along the frame) horizontal four with a single-plate clutch and shaft drive to the rear wheel. This novel longitudinal mounting of the entire drive-train provided an even lower centre of gravity than the original Boxer twin, yet kept the crank's rotational axis in the direction of travel, so the shaft absorbed less power. Looking down on the bike, one side of the engine carried the exhausts, while the other side consisted of the double overhead cams and their two valves per cylinder, on top of which was mounted the Bosch Jetronic fuel-injection system.

The genius of the K100RS was that its designers had managed to replace the unique Boxer system with a thoroughly modern solution which was still unmistakably a BMW. The new bike, like the old, had massive torque at the low end of the rpm scale, yet, unlike the original R100RS, the K could rev onwards towards 8500 rpm, where the maximum power of 90 bhp peaked, prompting a top speed of 125 mph and a standing quarter of a little over 12 seconds.

Elegant, suave and noble as it was, the bike had faults aplenty. Perhaps the biggest tragedy was that in attempting to emulate the Boxer's 'Captain Sensible' role as a mature sports/tourer, BMW compromised the excellent power-plant with dated and inappropriate suspension, notably the very soft and flexible front fork, without either adjustment or anti-dive, and the unacceptably grabby

front brakes, which had simply fallen behind the level of sophistication apparent on comparable Oriental machinery. BMW's answer was that any further complication in suspension was superfluous, but a fast ride over anything but the smoothest of surfaces proved this argument fallacious. At 588 lb fully fueled, the K100RS clearly demanded a more progressive and sophisticated suspension system than was necessary on its 450 lb predecessor. The shortcomings of the suspension were all the more disappointing because, in terms of pure steering, the bike performed superbly.

Moreover, the predecessor of the K100RS had built up a reputation as *the* all-year-round road bike because of its ingeniously-crafted fairing, which combined unrivalled weather protection with superb looks and finish. The new bike failed heavily in this respect, affording little more protection than the average handlebar-mounted bikini fairing, which proved unacceptable to most BMW lovers.

However, rumours of a 16-valve version of the 1000 cc power-plant mean that we may yet see a true sports version of BMW's fascinating new design.

BMW K100RS

Engine:	Longitudinally-mounted water-cooled horizontal in-line four	*Front brake:*	Twin 285 mm discs
		Rear brake:	Single 285 mm disc
Capacity:	987 cc	*Tyres:*	Metzeler perfect: 100/90V18 front,
Bore × stroke:	67 × 70 mm		130/90V17 rear
Compression ratio:	10.2:1	*Wheelbase:*	1516 mm
Carburation:	Bosch Jetronic fuel injected	*Rake/trail:*	53 degrees/4.13 in.
Power:	90 bhp @ 8000 rpm	*Weight:*	495 lb (dry)
Torque:	63 ft/lb @ 6000 rpm	*Fuel tank:*	4.8 gallons
Chassis:	Tubular space-frame with engine as stressed member	*Top speed:*	133.5 mph
		Standard quarter:	12.25 sec
Front suspension:	Telescopic fork (185 mm of travel)	*Fuel consumption:*	48 mpg
Rear suspension:	Mono leaver fork with single shock adjustable for three-position preload	*Range:*	225 miles

Suzuki RG250 Gamma

Ten years ago, a superbike review would hardly dare mention a 250 for fear of derisive laughter. In the days prior to 1982, a 250 was merely a pedestrian and often downright gutless appliance useful only to pass a riding test on. As soon as this had been accomplished, any self-respecting enthusiast would have passed on to a capacity at least twice that size.

However, despite the atrophy that may have occurred in the British 250 market and for whatever reasons, it is still the most hotly-contested capacity class in Japan, with a market size equal to the total British annual sales. So it was no surprise to learn of Suzuki's entry into the late-1983 mêlée, the RG250 Gamma, a closely-derived, half-size replica of Franco Uncini's world-championship-winning

1982 500 race bike, producing an astonishing and hitherto undreamt-of 45 bhp from its water-cooled parallel-twin engine. This propelled the new 250 road bike to an incredible 113 mph with later 1985 versions capable of nudging well past 120. That represented an amazing 50 per cent power increase over British 250s of 13 or 14 years before, and brought the $\frac{1}{4}$-litre class up to the levels of performance that 750s were achieving in 1969–70.

The secret behind the phenomenal new Suzuki lay not in its rather old-fashioned (if highly-tuned), two-stroke case-reed engine, but in its race-replica, all-aluminium, box-section chassis. Fabricated from HE30 aircraft-specification alloy, the

compact formation featured a full double-cradle and straight rails from swing-arm pivots to heavily-braced steering head, plus forged-aluminium rear-suspension and swinging-arm mounts. Rear full-floater suspension was all-alloy, too, and butch 35 mm front forks featured separate-leg air suspension and anti-dive. Brakes, with single-opposed pistons, could have been taken straight from the factory's racing bikes.

With a 16 in. front wheel, punching this low, light (less than 300 lb) and compact motorcycle through the air was little problem for the wicked, if rather peaky, high-compression engine. True, nothing much occurred below 7000 rpm, and the tachometer supplied by the factory did not even start reading until 3000 rpm, but when the power arrived, it was well worth the lack of torque lower down. Acceleration was more appropriate to a race bike than a 250 road machine. Surprisingly, little cost had to be paid for this performance in terms of either drive-train smoothness or general sophistication. The Gamma felt perfectly ridable on all terrain.

Not only did it feel ridable, but also stable beyond all expectation for a machine of this weight and size, with beautifully balanced suspension and incredibly light and precise steering. The RG proved the worth of anti-dive as an aid to fast cornering on bikes that were light enough to respond, rather than as an affectation on overweight hulks whose massive weight transference obviated the benefits. Fitted with Michelin TG race-tread tyres as original equipment, the Gamma could hardly be bettered along a twisty road, and it was not long before the first few filtered through to domestic UK road racing, where they soon began to dominate their class.

In 1986, the RG, despite Honda's ill-fated MVX250, Yamaha's RZ250 and Kawasaki's KR250 (none of which found its way to Britain), remained at the top of the pile. By then, the bike had a full fairing and twin discs, and it would have needed an exceptional motorcycle to break the Suzuki's three-year period of $\frac{1}{4}$-litre domination.

Suzuki RG250 Gamma

Engine:	Liquid-cooled case-reed two-stroke parallel twin	Front brake:	Single dual-opposed-piston caliper with 270 mm disc
Capacity:	247 cc	Rear brake:	Single dual-opposed-piston caliper with 210 mm disc
Bore × stroke:	54 × 54 mm	Tyres:	Dunlop F14/K130: 100/90-16-54S front, 100/90-18-56S rear
Compression ratio:	7.5:1		
Carburation:	Two 28 mm flat-slide Mikuni	Wheelbase:	1385 mm (54.5 in.)
Power:	45 ps @ 8500 rpm	Rake/trail:	61.25 degrees/4 in.
Torque:	27.4 ft/lb @ 8000 rpm	Weight:	288 lb (dry)
Chassis:	Light-alloy box-section duplex cradle frame	Fuel tank:	3.7 gallons
		Top speed:	113 mph (later model 119 mph)
Front suspension:	Telescopic air fork with anti-dive	Standard quarter:	13.7 sec
Rear suspension:	Alloy swing arm coupled with single shock linkage and remote preload adjustment	Fuel consumption:	40 mpg
		Range:	150 miles

Harris Magnum III

Despite the death of the UK motorcycle industry, or at least its long illness, one company that refused to succumb to the British disease of sitting on one's laurels was the small, family-run business of Harris Motorcycles in Hertford. Harris had become involved in bike building in much the same way as the original Bimota conspirators, and their success in designing and constructing competitive chassis for endurance and Formula 1 racing led them to offer frame kits for road use, too.

The so-called Magnums I and II were heavily-based replicas of the company's endurance chassis, designed for a number of engine options from the three major four-stroke transverse-four manufacturers. Although they handled, steered and performed with the precision of pukka racing tackle (and were, by the way, enormously successful as road bikes both in the UK and abroad), they lacked the comfort and reliability of mass-produced machinery, and the sheer style and finish of their Italian counterparts, Bimota. In 1984, when their frames carried Barry Sheene to fifth place in the world 500 cc championship (the first non-works bike home), no one doubted

the integrity of their design. Now, they needed a bike that put rider comfort and reliability as high on its list of priorities as performance and handling. Thus, the brief for the Magnum III was laid out.

It is ironic that, although they set about designing the new bike with such considerations paramount, Harris actually ended up producing their best *performing* road bike to date. Stylistically and ergonomically, the Magnum III was such a revelation, compared to its predecessors, that it is hard to believe the bikes could have been in any way associated. However, in essence, their basic principles were identical.

Fabricated from standard Reynolds 531 tubing instead of exotic, box-section aluminium (as was Barry Sheene's race frame) and manganese-bronze welded at every joint, the Magnum III's full double-cradle featured a 62.75-degree head angle and 127 mm of trail that was identical to their enormously successful 1984 F1 mounts. With an aluminium box-section rear swinging arm and large Avional support plates, which carried swing-arm pivot, top engine mount, top suspension mount and rocker-arm pivot, it is not difficult to see where the inspiration for Harris' modernization programme came from. Lockheed calipers, Forcella 40 mm front forks and a rising-rate rear monoshock completed the plot, which boasted a mere 29 in. seat height (2 in. less than the Magnum II) and a dry weight of only 450 lb, including the colossal GPz1100 engine.

As with Bimota, available power-plants were always a year behind existing development, although either the Kawasaki or Suzuki 1100 mills (and the 750 Turbo) could be slotted into the Magnum III chassis. Thus, performance was not absolute, but 150 mph plus was taken for granted, and the Harris could be built to be literally as fast as the particular owner's wallet would allow. With the fuel-injected Kawasaki 1100 motor, the bike felt creamily smooth and suffered none of the drive-train lash of earlier Magnums nor the drive-train harshness of the Bimota HB3 and SB4.

However, like the last two machines, it was handling, not ultimate engine performance, that separated the Harris from its mass-produced Japanese imitators. Low-speed steering was faultless, and total chassis/suspension wallow was negligible. Equipped with race-compound Pirelli Phantoms, it was a whole year later before Suzuki's GSX750R provided more grip, and only an international racer could have separated the Harris from comparable Bimotas.

Faults? Only the Lockheed calipers and the paintwork let it down, but at £3000 cheaper than its Italian equivalent, it was a truly remarkable achievement.

Harris Magnum III

Engine:	Kawasaki 1100, Suzuki 1100 (both dohc transverse fours). Specification relates to GPz1100 Kawasaki	*Rear suspension:*	White Power monoshock with damping and preload adjustment
		Front brake:	Twin Lockheed opposed-piston calipers with 280 mm Brembo discs
Capacity:	1089 cc	*Rear brake:*	Single Brembo with 260 mm disc
Bore × stroke:	72.5 × 66 mm	*Tyres:*	Pirelli Phantom 120/70V16 front, 170/70V16 rear
Compression ratio:	9.5:1		
Carburation:	Digital fuel injection	*Wheelbase:*	1460 mm
Power:	120 ps @ 8750 rpm	*Rake/trail:*	62.75 degrees/5 in.
Torque:	73.5 ft/lb @ 8000 rpm	*Weight:*	460 lb (dry)
Chassis:	Tubular double-cradle frame	*Fuel tank:*	Not available
Front suspension:	Forcella 40 mm forks or 42 mm Marzocchi MIR adjustable for preload and damping	*Top speed:*	150 mph
		Standard quarter:	Not available
		Fuel consumption:	40 mpg
		Range:	180 miles (approximately)

Kawasaki GPz900R

The class of 1984 ended still being dominated by the bike it had begun with—the Kawasaki GPz900R Ninja. Launched to the press in California at the end of 1983, the GPz900R instantly converted Yamaha's hitherto sports FJ1100 to a sports/tourer, and made nonsense of Honda's claim that you had to spend £5000 to own the fastest road bike. With a genuine top speed of over 155 mph and the most efficient power-to-weight ratio in its class, the Ninja was simply the finest all-round production sports bike ever built.

Basically, Kawasaki had to throw away the rule book in wresting the performance crown with a mere 900. By opting for a higher power-to-weight ratio and good aerodynamics, and designing the engine and chassis as an integrated package rather than as separate units with brute power and strength, Kawasaki was to establish a trend that is still the dominant theme in big-bike production. The engine, a water-cooled, 16-valve transverse four, was, at 16 in. across, the narrowest ever conceived for such a capacity. This was achieved by moving the cam chain from the centre of the four cylinders to the extreme left-hand side of the cylinder head. The incredibly compact power-plant was used as a stressed member in Kawasaki's all-new

diamond-shaped steel frame, keeping frontal area and machine height and weight to an absolute minimum.

The designers insisted on the most sophisticated and versatile suspension ever fitted to a production sports bike, with remarkably firm yet progressive air-adjustable front forks (also with four-position anti-dive adjustment) and a very smooth (if slightly soft) version of their established Uni-Trak rising-rate system at the rear. The new single-opposed-piston disc brakes adopted for the Ninja were also extremely powerful in the time-honoured Kawasaki tradition, but also exuded progression in a fashion never achieved on the company's previous big bikes. Moreover, the bike's dimensions and layout lent themselves to the most stylish full fairing seen on a road bike since BMW introduced the RS fairing in 1976. The 900 was razor-sharp in every respect.

It was this combination of the 900's assets, rather than any one particular feature, which led it literally to swamp the opposition in production racing. The bike steered impeccably at all speeds, was much more agile than anything in its class, and its only suspect component, the rear shock, could be replaced. On the road, this rear unit was perfectly adequate, and no other mass-produced, large-capacity four-stroke could hope to emulate the 900's all-round behaviour. Its awesome, cumulative and progressive power curve may not have been the most inspiring experience in motorcycling, but it was undeniably the most flexible, versatile and reliable in a variety of weather conditions. Moreover, the engine, though smooth, possessed an invigorating rawness of delivery, not unlike a European bike, while the transmission, like the instruments, electrics and ergonomics, was flawless. Even as a touring bike, the Ninja performed without vice, giving a 200-mile-plus range (far in excess of the FJ1100 or the Honda VF1000F) and providing exemplary comfort from its compromise of racing and touring riding position. In terms of pure road behaviour, hardly a word was, or could be, said against it.

All the 900's shortcomings were related to its record on reliability. Though Kawasaki were slow to admit it, the first batch of 900s was blighted with the same sort of cam-chain tensioner problems that had been an epidemic on Honda's earlier CX500 and CBX550. A limited number also suffered big-end failure, and all GPz900Rs were prone to overheating and starter-motor problems. But the blemishes could not tarnish a masterpiece. The Kawasaki was to reign supreme as the best all-rounder until late 1986.

Kawasaki GPz900R

Engine:	Water-cooled dohc 16-valve four-stroke four	Rear suspension:	Uni-Trak adjustable for damping and preload
Capacity:	908 cc	Front brake:	Twin 280 mm discs
Bore × stroke:	72.5 × 55 mm	Rear brake:	Single 270 mm disc
Compression ratio:	11:1	Tyres:	Dunlop F17:120/80V16 front,
Carburation:	Four 34 mm Keihin CV		130/80V18 rear
Power:	115 ps @ 9500 rpm	Wheelbase:	1495 mm
Torque:	62.9 ft/lb @ 8500 rpm	Rake/trail:	61 degrees/4.48 in.
Chassis:	Tubular Diamond frame with engine as stressed member	Weight:	501 lb
		Fuel tank:	4.8 gallons
Front suspension:	39 mm air fork adjustable for preload, damping and three-position anti-dive	Top speed:	154 mph
		Standard quarter:	10.83 sec @ 122.5 mph
		Fuel consumption:	43.4 mpg
		Range:	200 miles

Kawasaki GPz600

As if Kawasaki were not content with dominating the big-bike market in 1984, their introduction in December of the 'half-Ninja' GPz600 was confirmation that their engineers were on the crest of a technological wave and hoped to consolidate Kawasaki's reputation as the most important builders of four-stroke sports machinery.

In fact, the new 600 owed very little to either the chassis design or engine layout of the 900.

Furthermore, it raised Japanese styling to a new level of innovation and sophistication. However, it did borrow heavily from the general principles of the Ninja, with the emphasis on compactness, a good power-to-weight ratio and superb aerodynamics. Like the larger bike's power-plant, the engine was a liquid-cooled, dohc, 16-valve four-stroke with a similar transverse layout, but with the cam chain in its traditional position between

the centre cylinders. Centrally-sited plugs and a compression ratio of 11:1 gave the 600 an impressive 75 bhp and pushed the bike to a top speed that was comfortably beyond 130 mph—something 750s were only just attaining a year earlier.

Again, like the 900, this achievement was not due entirely to brute power but, more importantly, to low weight, with lightweight alloys and plastics being used wherever possible in both the engine and frame. The 600 seemed to borrow more heavily from Yamaha's FJ1100 than it did from its own stablemate, comprising as it did a full box-section steel cradle with a top-rail perimeter construction and a box-section aluminium swinging arm. Like the entire Kawasaki four-stroke

sporting range, the 600 featured damping and preload-adjustable Uni-Trak rear suspension and AVDS telescopic forks, which were virtually identical to the 900's. Twin single-piston discs up front and a single identical unit at the rear also aped those of its big brother.

The $\frac{1}{2}$-litre class had seen a decade of remarkable development; first with Honda's 1981 CBX550, then Suzuki's 1983 GSX550, and, again, Honda's 1984 VF500, all pushing real top speeds towards the magic 125 mph figure. But Kawasaki's mini-Ninja was both a qualitative and quantitative step forward, and it stamped its authority on the class with all the legitimacy of divinity. It possessed *genuine* 130 mph-plus performance, but more than that, it exhibited a continuity and smoothness of

Kawasaki GPz600

Engine:	Liquid-cooled 16-valve four-stroke four	Front brake:	Twin opposed-piston calipers with 280 mm discs
Capacity:	592 cc	Rear brake:	Single opposed-piston caliper with 270 mm disc
Bore × stroke:	60 × 52.4 mm		
Compression ratio:	11:1	Tyres:	Dunlop 110/90V16 front, 130/90V16 rear
Carburation:	Four 32 mm Keihin CV		
Power:	75 ps @ 9500 rpm	Wheelbase:	1430 mm
Torque:	38.3 ft/lb @ 9000 rpm	Rake/trail:	63 degrees/3.8 in.
Chassis:	Box-section perimeter steel double-cradle frame	Weight:	455 lb (full tank)
		Fuel tank:	4 gallons
Front suspension:	37 mm air fork with adjustable preload and three-position anti-dive	Top speed:	135 mph
		Standard quarter:	12.1 sec
Rear suspension:	Uni-Trak monoshock with infinitely-variable preload adjustment and four-position damping adjustment	Fuel consumption:	49 mpg
		Range:	195 miles

performance that was almost unique in its class. The engine was peaky, yet at the same time progressive, the gearbox and other drive-train components silky-smooth in operation. Handling was without equal in its class, a combination of quick steering via the 16 in. front wheel and precisely-tuned suspension which, like the 900, demonstrated progression and compliance without any loss of control. Perhaps only the excellent VF500 could stay with it over any protracted series of turns, but the 600 cc Kawasaki would have left the VF for dead along the straights in between.

Though it may have been a bit of a perch for taller riders, and offered far less in the way of protection than the original Ninja, the 600 proved every bit as versatile and popular as the bigger bike. It sold to the virtual exclusion of all else in the 1985 and 1986 sub-750 cc category, and gave Kawasaki the lead in every category over 125 cc in the British domestic motorcycle market during 1986. At the end of that year, the 600 still dominated the mid-weight category, and only Honda's newly-announced CB600 threatened. Rumour had it that Kawasaki had an even more potent, all-aluminium-framed version ready to counter that threat.

Yamaha FZ750

With so much of 1984's genius going into the building of strokers, Kawasaki's GPz900R was having an untroubled time at the top of the four-stroke pile. Thus the launch of Yamaha's FZ750 came as a genuine shock to the whole motorcycle world. So much of the bike was truly innovative that it was difficult to take it all in at one go.

Developed, like Kawasaki's four-stroke fours, as an integrated chassis/engine concept, the idea behind the FZ750 was to gain the lowest possible centre of mass by canting the transverse-four engine 45 degrees from the vertical towards the front of the machine. This allowed direct, vertical draughts from the intake system to the inlet side of the engine and, in turn, the fuel reservoir was allowed to occupy the position vacated by the carburettors. But the real pinnacle of this combustion technology was in Yamaha's adoption of five valves per cylinder, three inlet and two exhaust, making the FZ750 the world's first 20-valve motorcycle engine.

The theory behind the extra inlet valve was simply that three small holes could pass more mixture more efficiently than two big holes.

Moreover, being smaller and lighter, the valves possessed less inertia and raised the mechanical limits of the entire cam-train, allowing the engine to be revved higher—apparently, the first prototype FZ produced 130 bhp at 13,000 rpm. Multi-valving also helped to improve combustion-chamber shape, which, in conjunction with slightly dished pistons, a centrally located plug and an impressive 11.2:1 compression ratio, resulted in a spectacular 100 bhp at the crankshaft; cc for cc, it was some 10 bhp stronger than Kawasaki's GPz900R.

It was not just the extra power from the five-valve cylinder technology that was impressive; rather it was the range of that power which was unparalleled in any other machine of its capacity. Roll the throttle off right down to 1500 rpm in top, then crack it open and the bike would still pull away cleanly, strongly and purposefully; drop down three cogs and wind the throttle open at 7000 rpm plus, and things would really move, fast enough for an $11\frac{1}{2}$-second quarter and a top speed of around 148 mph.

If the engine was exhilarating, then the chassis was simply intoxicating, allowing the FZ to be hurled deep into corners with the brakes hard on, not unlike the new breed of lightweight two-strokes. Once again, low centre of mass, low steering-head height and plenty of engine weight over the front wheel must take most of the credit for this characteristic. Similarly, the steel, box-section perimeter frame (detachable at the front for engine removal) allowed the FZ's 460 lb to be tilted over to the limits of tyre adhesion, and then some. Hang off it a bit and you were really moving. Preload- and damping-adjustable rear monocross suspension and air-assisted, but anti-dive-free, short front forks sustained the sensation of thoroughbred sporting firmness, but were pliant enough to allow comfortable, exciting, long-distance touring. Though admirably progressive, the only parts of the chassis that could have done with more of anything were the brakes which, though adequate, when compared to the Suzuki GSX or the Ninja seemed somewhat spongy.

However, stability was really the FZ's hallmark. Given the 16 in. front wheel, the radical chassis design and the high-tech nature of the engine, you would be forgiven for not expecting it. But Yamaha had seen the success of the Ninja and they were keen to have some. Disappointingly, although the FZ won every accolade in every magazine in every country and despite achieving notable victories in the prestigious UK Superstock series, its sales flopped in 1985. It took until 1986 for the public's imagination to catch up with Yamaha's.

Yamaha FZ750

Engine:	Water-cooled four-stroke	*Front brake:*	Twin 270 mm discs with opposed-piston calipers
Capacity:	749 cc		
Bore × stroke:	68 × 51.6 mm	*Rear brake:*	Single 270 mm disc with opposed-piston caliper
Compression ratio:	11.2:1		
Carburation:	Four 34 mm Mikuni down-draught	*Tyres:*	Dunlop 120/80 16 in. front, 130/80 18 in. rear
Power:	105 ps		
Torque:	61.5 ft/lb @ 8250 rpm	*Wheelbase:*	1485 mm
Chassis:	Box-section double-cradle perimeter frame	*Rake/trail:*	65.5 degrees/3.7 in.
		Weight:	410 lb (dry)
Front suspension:	Telescopic air-assisted fork	*Fuel tank:*	4.8 gallons
Rear suspension:	Monocross monoshock with five-way preload adjustment and five-way damping adjustment	*Top speed:*	149 mph
		Standard quarter:	11.2 sec @ 120 mph
		Fuel consumption:	38 mpg
		Range:	180 miles

Suzuki GSX750R

While Yamaha took the high road to super-performance motorcycling, Suzuki opted for the comparatively low, traditional route to increased power. Searching for competitiveness within their existing range of engines, Suzuki's engineers identified weight saving in the chassis and engine as the route to 750 world domination. Thus, they took inspiration from their own Honda-beating race bikes, but for production, had to find a slimming programme that would keep the new GSX750R's weight below the magic 400 lb barrier.

Eschewing water-cooling as being too heavy, Suzuki adopted oil-cooling as a means of reducing cylinder-head temperatures and, thus, were able to reduce the weight of reciprocating components. They succeeded brilliantly, keeping temperatures to around 100 degrees Celsius and reducing the weight of the fully-lubricated motor by some 50 lb compared to the original GSX750. The dohc in-line four had 16 valves and Suzuki's TSCC (twin-swirl combustion chambers). Although the bore and stroke had been opened up to 70 × 48.7 mm,

compression raised to 10.6:1, both inlet and exhaust valve sizes increased and timing lengthened, in essence, the motor was still the same as the GSX launched in 1980. Now, however, it boasted 105 bhp instead of 85 bhp and weighed 160 lb, not 210 lb.

Sustaining the same theme for the chassis was never much of a problem, the box-section, full-cradle construction being fashioned entirely from case and extruded aluminium and incorporating a light-alloy swing arm and a rear shock that was slightly more upright than the GSX750E's. Preload-adjustable front forks with anti-dive featured twin-opposed-piston discs, yet retained 18 in. wheels front and back. With the complete bike weighing in at around 388 lb, a 16 in. wheel might have proved too skittish. As it was, despite being a superb handler and cleaning up in the 1985 Superstock production series, the GSX750R manifested a high-speed wobble. This mattered little on the track, where ideal conditions and the modifications allowed on racing machines negated the effect. However, on the road, where poor conditions and inexperience often conspired together, the new sports 750 could be a real handful.

That did not stop the gawdy, brash 'racer with lights' outselling every other 750 in 1985, and in normal conditions no other ¾-litre production bike could compete with its combination of ultra-low weight, phenomenal cornering grip and outstanding performance. It was a true racer straight from the crate, with many competitors successfully campaigning bog-stock bikes from the showroom floor. The GSX became the only production bike for privateers, and its stranglehold on all production-based races, whether on short track or long, soon became absolute. Even seasoned racers such as Roger Marshall and Roger Burnett were heard to protest that racing their own production Honda VF750Rs was all but useless against the GSX750R because 'it's a real racer'.

Riding the Suzuki on the road was a different matter. Uncomfortable and uncompromising, power delivery was an all-or-nothing affair, with little on offer below 7000 rpm and the world instantly in reverse above it. Sensitive and unpredictable, it demanded undivided attention from even the most experienced of riders. And, of course, there was the dreaded weave. By the time the latter was diagnosed as a symptom of too short a swing arm and rectified, the GSX was past the peak of its sales. Even so, it remained the dominant 750 until the end of 1986, and had established a general trend for Suzuki's four-stroke sports bikes.

Suzuki GSX750R

Engine:	Dohc 16-valve oil-cooled four-stroke four	Front brake:	Twin dual-opposed-piston calipers with 300 mm discs
Capacity:	749 cc	Rear brake:	Single dual-opposed-piston caliper with 220 mm disc
Bore × stroke:	70 × 48.7 mm		
Compression ratio:	10.6:1	Tyres:	Bridgestone 18 in. front, 18 in. rear
Carburation:	Four flat-slide Mikuni	Wheelbase:	1435 mm
Power:	100 ps @ 10,500 rpm	Rake/trail:	64 degrees/4.25 in.
Torque:	55 ft/lb @ 9000 rpm	Weight:	395 lb
Chassis:	Extruded aluminium box-section double-cradle frame	Fuel tank:	4.2 gallons
		Top speed:	149 mph
Front suspension:	40 mm telescopic fork with four-way preload adjustment and four-position anti-dive	Standard quarter:	11.2 sec @ 122.6 mph
		Fuel consumption:	28 mpg
		Range:	120 miles
Rear suspension:	Full-floater monoshock and four-way damping adjustment		

Suzuki RG500 Gamma

While Yamaha had traditionally been the market leaders in two-stroke technology, the success of Suzuki's RG250 and the enormous pre-launch publicity accorded to the RD500 prompted Suzuki into designing and building their own full-blown 500 to contest what they assumed to be a lucrative sports bike market. Thus, at the Cologne Show in September 1984, Suzuki unveiled their RG500 Gamma, a bike they optimistically declared would trounce the RD500 in every department.

The reason for such corporate confidence was clear once the new $\frac{1}{2}$-litre's vital statistics were analysed; 95 bhp instead of the RD's 85 bhp, pushing 340 lb instead of the Yamaha's 390 lb. True, Suzuki's job was much easier, for Yamaha had been left to test the market, while the former merely had to add more power and subtract more weight from the Yamaha equation. However, in

retrospect, the manner in which Suzuki achieved this goal did make some areas of the Yamaha's development look tacky. The Suzuki oozed quality from headlight to tail lens, and it was obvious that there were no grey areas of development left in the rush to get this bike out.

Despite being an altogether better road bike than the RD, the Gamma borrowed much more heavily from its racing counterpart than the Yamaha did from the YZR500. In keeping with both Barry Sheene's and Franco Uncini's championship-winning bikes of 1976 and 1982, the engine comprised a square-four two-stroke with a stepped crank for ultimate compactness. The original 1970s race bike's bore and stroke of 54 × 54 mm were modified to 56 × 50 mm for road use, and the racer's disc valves with AEC retained. AEC was Suzuki's version of the power valve, a device

pioneered by Yamaha which alters exhaust-port timing at different rpm for optimum power and response.

Equipped with four 28 mm flat-sided carburettors, the engine produced maximum power of 95 bhp at 9500 rpm and maximum torque at 9000 rpm. This massive power step at around 8000 rpm made the RG500's power delivery probably the most exhilarating on the road and the closest sensation to a racer that any road rider was likely to experience. Not only did it make the RG insanely quick in the hands of a skilled rider, but it also made the bike frighteningly wild in the hands of novices. Even experienced riders were heard to mumble their anxiety about being able to ride the bike in the 'sweet spot'—that is, make the most of its huge performance and handling parameters by riding it close to its limits like a pukka race machine, where the RG rewarded the rider most richly.

That is not to say the bike was not versatile; it was almost embarrassingly good at anything from city commuting to continental touring. Its light weight gave in-town agility and its smooth power delivery and excellent riding position made cross-country bolts tireless. But what was the point of the all-aluminium box-section frame, the 16 in. front and 17 in. rear wheels, the anti-dive, air-assisted front fork and the full-floater, box-section rear suspension if it was not for riding insanely fast through corners? Beautifully controlled and firm rear damping (not unlike the Harris Magnum), and the ease of controlling and transferring the bike's minimal weight, made even the sensational new four-stroke GPz600 seem ponderous by comparison. The RG500 could be ridden in deeper and powered out harder than almost any other motorcycle on the UK market. It was a jet, and like a jet could lift its front wheel without hesitation.

Sadly, Suzuki had misread the market. The Yamaha RD500 had satisfied both the enthusiasts' limited demand and the public's curiosity; the RG500 arrived too late to make any headway. As a consequence, it never sold well.

Suzuki RG500 Gamma

Engine:	Liquid-cooled two-stroke square four	*Front brake:*	Twin dual-opposed-piston calipers with 260 mm floating discs
Capacity:	498 cc	*Rear brake:*	Single dual-opposed-piston caliper with 210 mm disc
Bore × stroke:	56 × 50.6 mm		
Compression ratio:	7:1	*Tyres:*	Michelin 110/90V16 front, 120/90V18 rear
Carburation:	Four 28 mm flat-slide Mikuni		
Power:	95 ps @ 9500 rpm	*Wheelbase:*	1425 mm
Torque:	42.8 ft/lb @ 9000 rpm	*Rake/trail:*	64 degrees/4.4 in.
Chassis:	Extruded box-section aluminium double-cradle frame	*Weight:*	340 lb (dry)
		Fuel tank:	4.8 gallons
Front suspension:	38 mm air-assisted fork with variable compression damping	*Top speed:*	150 mph (estimated)
		Standard quarter:	Not available
		Fuel consumption:	30 mpg
Rear suspension:	Full-floater monoshock with hydraulically-variable preload	*Range:*	145 miles

Kawasaki GPz1000RX

By late 1985, with their hitherto unassailable GPz900R two years old, Kawasaki could not resist the urge to build a full 1000 cc version of the all-conquering four-stroke. Anxious to maintain absolute dominance in the big sports bike category and conscious that in the 900 every other manufacturer had a target to aim at, Kawasaki sought to usurp those threats with the GPz1000RX before they even got off the ground. Ironically, the plan backfired completely, for in attempting to build a machine for out-and-out top speed, Kawasaki had undone every piece of good work they had achieved with the Ninja. However satisfactory its short-term sales, the bike did not overwhelm the press, and the long-term future of the design was called into question.

There was no argument with the theory; a bored-out Ninja seemed just the job. The latter's bore and stroke were stretched to 74 × 58 mm, new flat-top pistons, rings and gudgeon pins installed, the compression ratio lowered and considerable revisions made to the intake system. Increased dimensions required a stronger crankshaft, big-end bolts and conrods. Rubber engine mounts were also necessary, and the 900's weak points, namely starter motor, clutch and cooling system, were all either strengthened or revised.

These revisions lifted power from the 900's 116 bhp to a new total of 125 bhp, and there were no arguments over the improvement. Apart from an appalling glitch at 3500 rpm, the 1000 not only pushed top speed on another 7–8 mph to a genuine

160 mph plus and dismissed the quarter-mile in 0.2 seconds less than the smaller bike, but it improved ridability all the way through the rev range. Gone was the Ninja's rawness of delivery, to be replaced by a silky smoothness; banished was the 900's somewhat tedious, cumulative power delivery, to be succeeded by a motor with both real torque low down and real teeth high up. The bigger bike was

better everywhere you chose to open the throttle.

It was a tragedy that the extra weight could not be contained by a more suitable chassis. The diamond-shaped steel backbone frame of the 900, which used the smaller motor as a stressed frame member, was ditched due to its apparent (but slightly unbelievable) inadequacy in the face of the RX's extra 10 bhp. More likely is that the box-

section steel perimeter frame, used on the 1000 in its stead, had been made indispensably fashionable by both Yamaha's FJ1100 and Kawasaki's own GPz600. Leaving black tubes where black rectangles were considered *de rigueur* may have been tempting market fate.

Despite the similarity of suspension ingredients on both bikes, identical-specification brakes, and the single difference of a 16 in. rear wheel instead of an 18 in. version on the 1000, the latter had lost all the poise, agility and balance of its smaller stablemate. Although it handled acceptably near its limits, it could not be relied upon for the same neutrality of steering or ease of turning that the Ninja provided. Sometimes it felt positively dumpy, with an awkward sit-on riding position instead of the 900's sit-in feel, and where surfaces were not perfect or smoothness and continuity of approach could not be maintained, the 1000 began to roll round its axis. Put simply, it could not be abused like the 900, would never have got round a series of turns in the same time and simply was not as much fun to ride. It also possessed a poor fuel range and a wildly inaccurate gauge.

The 1000RX, accomplished superbike though it was, was simply a rush job. Three months later, Suzuki's GSX1100R showed it could be done.

Kawasaki GPz1000RX

Engine:	Water-cooled 16-valve transverse four-stroke four	Rear suspension:	Uni-Trak adjustable for preload and damping
Capacity:	997 cc	Front brake:	Twin 280 mm single-piston discs
Bore × stroke:	74 × 58 mm	Rear brake:	Single 270 mm disc
Compression ratio:	10.2:1	Tyres:	Dunlop F17/K725: 120/80V16 front, 150/80V16 rear
Carburation:	Four 36 mm Keihin CVK		
Power:	125 bhp	Wheelbase:	1505 mm
Torque:	73.1 ft/lb @ 8500 rpm	Rake/trail:	62 degrees/4.25 in.
Chassis:	Steel box-section double-cradle perimeter frame	Weight:	238 kg (526 lb) dry
		Fuel tank:	4.6 gallons (21 litres)
Front suspension:	Telescopic 40 mm air fork adjustable for preload, damping and three-position anti-dive	Top speed:	162 mph
		Standard quarter:	11 sec @ 124 mph
		Fuel consumption:	34 mpg
		Range:	155 miles

Honda NS400

With Honda still licking their wounds after their abdication from the four-stroke big-bike market, their nervousness at getting dragged into a two-stroke GP replica war and *losing* was understandable. For this reason, they announced to the world that they would be building a two-stroke replica of World Champion Freddie Spencer's GP bike, but that it would be a 400 rather than a full-blown 500 to avoid the inevitable power escalation that competing directly with Suzuki and Yamaha would bring. It was not so much that Honda wanted to save the world, rather that they thought they might lose the war.

At £3000, it was obvious that the bike would not be competing with Yamaha's bargain RD350, either. However, whether by luck or good

judgement, Honda managed to carve out a slice of the market all to themselves with the 400, and it sold much better than the ageing Yamaha or the more contemporary Suzuki. This was due, in no small measure, to the kudos of owning a bike that really did look like cult hero Freddie Spencer's GP mount. But what really prompted the success of the NS was that it handled like the race bike, too. It seemed as if Honda had taken the RG500's characteristics as a blueprint and then gone

further. For if the RG's handling was excellent, the 400's was better still. For once, the press were at one—this was probably the best-handling road bike *ever* built.

Once again, prudent weight-watching and compact dimensions were the major ingredients for success. The NS400's all-aluminium, duplex-cradle frame had a wheelbase of a mere 54.5 in., and steering on a 63-degree rake and 100 mm trail meant true race-replica agility and response to input. Compared to either the RG500 or the old RD350LC, the NS felt minute, the significantly smaller frontal area and excellent aerodynamics contributing substantially to its surprising performance.

Suspension, too, was beyond reproach, featuring colossal 37 mm air-assisted forks with TRAC anti-dive and the famed Pro-Link rising-rate monoshock with hydraulically-adjustable preload at the rear. The NS400 did not seem to have any limits. The steering was neutral and reacted to the slightest input; the suspension was precise, firm, progressive and actually variable; the brakes were faultless; and the only parameters that mattered were those dictated by the standard tyres and the fairing belly-pan. You could ride the bike at full tilt further than any other ½-litre machine, and expert riders could steer, as on a true racer, by sliding the rear tyre on long fast sweepers.

With genuine 130 mph-plus performance from 397 cc, it is ironic that the motor was not that powerful. Top speed itself came from a combination of low weight and excellent aerodynamics, rather than exceptional power. Although a replica of Freddie Spencer's two-stroke V3, the engine's cylinder configuration had actually been reversed on the NS so that two pots faced forward and the other towards the sky. Only the front two used the electronically-controlled ATAC system. Not surprisingly, transfer and exhaust ports were significantly different on the lower-capacity bike, too, and bore and stroke were reduced to 57 × 50.6 mm.

Like the RG500 Gamma, the NS was a peaky beast. A powerband effectively restricted to 2000 rpm and a torque curve which culminated even more severely meant a stiff left foot was the order of the day. The bike also displayed the most appalling fuel-consumption figures recorded on a superbike since the outrageous Kawasaki H1 triples of the early 1970s, with averages in the mid-20s being commonplace. Rich boy's toy? Maybe. But it sure was a lot of fun.

Honda NS400R

Engine:	Liquid-cooled two-stroke V3	Front brake:	Twin 256 mm dual-piston caliper
Capacity:	387 cc	Rear brake:	Not available
Bore × stroke:	57 × 50.6 mm	Tyres:	Bridgestone 100/90V16 front,
Compression ratio:	6.7:1		110/90V17 rear
Carburation:	Three 26 mm Keihin	Wheelbase:	1385 mm
Power:	51 bhp @ 9000 rpm	Rake/trail:	27 degrees/Not available
Torque:	32 ft/lb @ 8000 rpm	Weight:	359 lb (dry)
Chassis:	Aluminium box-section double-cradle frame	Fuel tank:	4.2 gallons
		Top speed:	132 mph
Front suspension:	37 mm air-assisted fork with TRAC anti-dive	Standard quarter:	Not available
		Fuel consumption:	30 mpg
Rear suspension:	Rising-rate Pro-Link with adjustable preload	Range:	125 miles

Suzuki GSX1100R

Suzuki's GSX1100R proved to be the antithesis of everything about the GPz1000RX. Not only was it an improvement on its predecessor, but it silenced once and for all the charge that large cylinder displacement and good handling were mutually exclusive properties. After all, this was the bike on which Trevor Nation lapped the Isle of Man TT course at over 113 mph, a mere 2 mph slower than Joey Dunlop's outright lap record of a couple of years before, which was achieved on a fully-kitted race TZ750.

The technology for the GSX1100R was pure GSX750R, boasting the same TSCC principles, identical 16-valve dohc layout and the innovative

oil-cooling arrangement which provided separate pumps for cylinder head and block. However, whereas the 750's 70 × 48.7 mm bore and stroke dimensions provided power that was absurdly peaky, the 1100's 76 × 58 mm internal boundaries

and lower compression ratio of 10:1 produced one of the flattest torque curves ever from Suzuki. This meant respectable pulling power from as little as 3000 rpm in top, colossal mid-range by 5000 and devastating response by the time the 1100 reached the 750's take-off point of 7000 rpm. Interestingly, although the big Kawasaki might have just pipped it flat out through the gears over the half-mile, the Suzuki easily wore the pants over the quarter (with a significant 0.2 seconds better performance) and also dominated the top-speed contest, with a best one-way recorded by one magazine of 168 mph!

This is not surprising really, when you consider the Suzuki's absurdly low weight of just over 440 lb, almost 1 cwt less than Yamaha's equivalent FJ1200. Combine this with a short first gear, and the 1100's impressive 127 bhp had no trouble lifting the front wheel (in truth, the main trouble was keeping it down).

As a sports bike, the impressive flexibility of the 1100's engine was demonstrated by the fact that it only gave away 0.2 seconds to the touring FJ1200 over the quarter-mile in a top-gear roll-on from 50 mph.

However, like the GSX750R and other class leaders before it, the 1100's real significance was in the combination of performance with the stunning abilities of the chassis. Fabricated almost exclusively from cast aluminium, the box-section, full-cradle perimeter frame established a control over the precocious motor that would have been deemed impossible two years previously. With an 18 in. front wheel, identical steering geometry to the 1986-specification 750, but with a slightly longer wheelbase, a stronger frame and wider tyres, the 1100 felt like a scaled-up $\frac{3}{4}$-litre bike with none of the original's handling idiosyncrasies. If ever a motorcycle fitted the phrase 'handles like on rails', this was it—that is exactly what it felt like. Implausible though it sounds, the 1100 actually steered with more response than the 200 cc slighter GPz900R; handled with more stability than the 350 cc lower GSX750R; and, in terms of overall precision, had no rivals at all. At the first attempt, Suzuki had established the 1100R as the fastest production bike ever, over any terrain. Suddenly, it became the benchmark against which others would be measured.

All these superlatives had a price, of course, like the measly 30 mpg and the infuriating 100-mile tank range. The GSX1100R also had a no-holds-barred, pure-racer riding position, and it could not be ridden in all situations with the same ease as the almost sedate, by comparison, GPz900R. But when the advantages of owning the fastest, best-handling, best-stopping superbike in production were considered, such inadequacies paled into insignificance.

Suzuki GSX1100R

Engine:	Oil-cooled 16-valve transverse four	Front brake:	Twin 310 mm (12 in.) discs (dual opposed-piston)
Capacity:	1052 cc	Rear brake:	Single 220 mm (8½ in.) disc (dual opposed-piston)
Bore × stroke:	76 × 58 mm		
Compression ratio:	10:1	Tyres:	Dunlop radials: 110/80V18 front,
Carburation:	Four 34 mm Mikuni flat-slide CV		150/70V18 rear
Power:	125 bhp	Wheelbase:	1460 mm
Torque:	74.5 ft/lb @ 8500 rpm	Rake/trail:	63.5 degrees/4.5 in.
Chassis:	Extruded aluminium box-section double-cradle frame	Weight:	436 lb (dry)
		Fuel tank:	5 gallons
Front suspension:	Telescopic 41 mm fork with preload adjustment and three-way anti-dive	Top speed:	165 mph
		Standard quarter:	10.8 sec @ 126 mph
Rear suspension:	Full-floater monoshock with preload and damping adjustment	Fuel consumption:	Not available
		Range:	125 miles

Honda VFR750

It was 1982 when Honda gave the world the first mass-produced V4 production motorcycle, and the 750S was met with all the enthusiasm one accords cold porridge. The revolutionary motor was compromised by appalling styling, appalling riding position and, frankly, appalling handling. One year later, however, Honda had set the record straight by turning the ugly-duckling VF750S into the VF750F nubile swan, a super-sports version of the original, which outsold every other 750. Unfortunately, the F was plagued by mechanical reliability problems, and by the time Honda had extended its V4 range to include a 500, a 1000, and a 1000 cc race-replica, the public had lost faith and imagination in the configuration.

Unused to being on the end of a market thrashing and aware of the huge market gains being made by Yamaha and Suzuki with their FZ750 and GSX750R respectively, Honda retreated to redesign their V4 range. It took until 1985 to get it right, by which time, although the Honda had been voted Bike of the Year in many quarters, the 750 market was dwindling irrevocably.

The VFR reversed all that when Ron Haslam, Honda Grand Prix rider and competitor extraordinaire, campaigned a standard showroom VFR to third place in the hotly-contested international Transatlantic race series. True, he was aided by both a wet track (which slowed the faster, pukka race bikes) and incredibly grippy race-compound tyres, but it was still an incredible achievement. As a consequence, Honda sold all of its annual allocation of VFRs on the following Monday!

Although developed from the doomed VF750FD and sharing identical internal dimensions of 70 × 48.6 mm bore and stroke and a 10.5:1 compression ratio, the new bike differed in the adoption of a 180-degree crank throw (instead of the FD's 360-degree arrangement), each cylinder firing separately, and like the VFR1000R from a year earlier,

incorporated gear-drive cams instead of chains. These clockwork-sounding units operated four valves per cylinder which, in turn, were fed by larger 34 mm CV carbs through much straighter inlet paths and tracts than the original. Of course, there were revisions to both the lubrication system and the camshaft-bearing housings to prevent any recurrence of the V-engine's earlier traumas.

The result of these improvements was a 20 per cent increase in power over the 750F with some 40 lb less to propel. Like all Honda's V4s, the VFR's endearing characteristics were the colossal torque at any rpm and its superb driveability out of corners. The 180-degree crank also gave the bike a harsher feel, and the power increase was most noticeable at around 8000 rpm, where the old bike died somewhat but the new one was just finding its

Honda VFR750

Engine:	Water-cooled 16-valve 90-degree V4	Rear brake:	Single dual-opposed-piston caliper with 256 mm disc
Capacity:	748 cc		
Bore × stroke:	70 × 40.6 mm	Tyres:	Dunlop 110/90V16 front, 130/80V18 rear
Compression ratio:	10.5:1		
Carburation:	Four 34 mm Keihin CV	Wheelbase:	1480 mm
Power:	100 ps @ 10,200 rpm	Rake/trail:	63 degrees/4.25 in.
Torque:	60 ft/lb @ 8500 rpm	Weight:	449 lb (including 1 gallon of fuel)
Chassis:	Twin-spar aluminium beam frame	Fuel tank:	4.4 gallons
Front suspension:	Air-assisted 37 mm fork with four-position anti-dive	Top speed:	150 mph
		Standard quarter:	11.7 sec @ 115 mph (estimated)
Rear suspension:	Pro-Link monoshock with infinitely-variable preload	Fuel consumption:	40 mpg
		Range:	180 miles
Front brake:	Twin dual-opposed-piston calipers with 276 mm discs		

legs. This gave the R a 148 mph top speed and a quarter-mile potential of a little over 11.5 seconds.

Once again, like all the successful superbikes of 1985, the VFR relied as much on the innovation of its chassis as it did on the engine. In a major departure from the F's earlier design, Honda opted for a simple rectangular-section, aluminium frame, the main feature of which was the direct run of the twin spars from steering head to swing-arm intersection. The latter was also made of aluminium, and the entire assembly weighed only 14 kg. At the rear, this was complemented by a preload-adjustable, Pro-Link rising-rate monoshock, and at the front by 37 mm air-adjustable telescopic forks with TRAC anti-dive on a single leg. These gave something of a soft ride, but on the whole suspension was excellent, and the twin-pot 276 mm front discs were the best in their class.

Of the three race-derived 750s, the Honda was by far the easiest to ride and easily the most competent all-rounder. Steering, via a 16 in. front wheel, was deceptively quick, and at 437 lb (about halfway between the Suzuki and the Yamaha) the VFR was uncannily manoeuvrable. It could change line midway through a corner with the minimum of fuss, scratch with the best of them, yet its seating position and fairing made it unique among the current 750s as an excellent touring mount as well. Not surprisingly, it soared to the top of the 750 sales charts.

Bimota DB1

Despite their superb quality and the incomparable performance of their chassis, selling Bimotas for £8000 gave the company a strictly limited life expectancy. When the Japanese proved they could build first-class frames as well, the market for Bimota's hand-assembled products dwindled still further. What they needed was a product with a broader appeal that would take them out of direct competition with Japan, yet would remain as unique and desirable as only a Bimota could.

The arrival of Federico Martini, who had worked under the legendary Taglioni on the new generation of Ducati V-engines, solved the problem in one swoop. The obvious answer to Bimota's model problem was to combine Italy's most prestigious engine with the country's most prestigious frame, an association that would not only encourage the all-Italian ethos but would also reduce logistical problems of supply and the economies of build. The resulting product, the 750

Pantah-engined DB1, proved so popular that it transformed Bimota virtually overnight from a small hand-assembly company fighting bankruptcy to a small-volume manufacturer whose order books and sales were assured for the next two years.

Much of the credit for this popularity must be attributed to the unique lines of the bike's bodywork, universally acclaimed as the most beautiful styling ever conceived for a motorcycle. But the stunning homogeneity of the tank/seat unit and the all-enveloping fairing provided function as

well as fashion, creating excellent aerodynamics and cooling by scooping air up and over the 90-degree V-twin engine.

The frame itself was a traditional Bimota design, comprising small, triangular structures in chrome-molybdenum from steering head to swing arm, from which the engine was suspended and acted as a stressed frame member. The only component made of box-section rather than tubing was the steel swing arm. This was augmented by a near-vertical, rising-rate Marzocchi shock, which was adjustable for rebound damping. At the other end, the Bimota adopted one of the most expensive and exotic-looking front ends ever fitted to a production motorcycle. It featured massive 41 mm four-way (compression-damping adjustable) Marzocchis with remote alloy master cylinders, compressed by Bimota's own Avional yokes. With the inclusion of fully-floating Brembo Goldline brakes and Bimota's glued and riveted three-spoke alloy wheels carrying Michelin radial tyres, it is not hard to see why Bimotas were so expensive. But they did exude quality from every nut and bolt.

On the track, with smooth surfaces and perfect curves, the Bimota was masterful, and even the Japanese factories found it hard to beat. On British roads, however, the DB1 was more of a handful than one might expect, mainly because front-end damping was so uncompromisingly hard and low-speed turning perhaps not as neutral as it could have been. With a meagre 61-degree rake, the Bimota still managed to steer incredibly swiftly, but it was not like the latest generation of Japanese sports bikes. With these, braking could be left to the last minute and the bike simply dropped into a turn. No, this was a bike built in the classic tradition, where lines had to be thought out and corners combined.

The similarly-engined Ducati F1, introduced to Britain at about the same time as the Bimota and making identical power, seemed to have the edge on the DB1 for road use. Both bikes incorporated standard versions of the bored-and-stroked 750 Pantah engine with desmodromic valve-gear operation and toothed-belt cam-gear drive. Both were capable of about 125 mph. But whatever edge it may have had in other areas, when it came to sheer style, there was simply no contest—the DB1 was the undisputed king.

Bimota DB1/Ducati F1

Engine:	Air-cooled 90-degree sohc V-twin	Air-cooled 90-degree sohc V-twin	Rear suspension:	Marzocchi monoshock with infinite preload and ten-position damping adjustment	Marzocchi monoshock with infinitely-adjustable preload
Capacity:	748 cc	748 cc			
Bore × stroke:	88 × 61.5 mm	88 × 61.5 mm			
Compression ratio:	9.3:1	9.3:1			
Carburation:	Two 36 mm Dell'Orto	Two 36 mm Dell'Orto	Front brake:	Twin 280 mm Brembo Goldline floating discs	Twin 280 mm Brembo Goldline floating discs
Power:	76 bhp @ 9000 rpm	76 bhp @ 9000 rpm			
Torque:	Not available	Not available	Rear brake:	Single 260 mm disc	Single 260 mm disc
Chassis:	Tubular steel space-frame with engine as stressed frame member	Tubular steel space-frame with engine as stressed member	Tyres:	Pirelli 130/60V16 front, 160/60V16 rear	Michelin 120/80V16 front, 130/80V18 rear
			Wheelbase:	1380 mm	1455 mm
Front suspension:	Marzocchi forks with compression-damping adjustment	40 mm Forcella forks with five-way preload and three-way damping adjustment	Rake/trail:	Not available	Not available
			Weight:	354 lb	385 lb
			Fuel tank:	4.4 gallons	3.5 gallons
			Top speed:	125 mph	125 mph (estimated)
			Standard quarter:	Not available	Not available
			Fuel consumption:	Not available	52 mpg
			Range:	Not available	180 miles

Ducati Paso

Although Ducati produced some remarkable superbikes in the first half of the 1980s, notably the 1982 Hailwood Replica and the 1985 750 cc Ducati F1, none caught the public's imagination quite like the sports/touring Paso launched in the autumn of 1986. Like the Bimota, it managed to combine the traditional virtues of its marque with an innovative departure in styling and ergonomics, made all the more remarkable because of the period of uncertainty its factory was going through. As if to mirror the Rimini company's experiences, the Paso looked set to turn the tide on Ducati's rather poor 1986 sales figures, just as the DB1 had done.

In fact, the experiences of the two factories were no mere coincidence. The incestuousness with which design staff moved between the factories during 1984–86 brought with it an inevitable similarity of ideas. Federico Martini, the man responsible for designing the DB1, had spent the previous six years at Ducati, and the man he

750 F1 Replica was the last Ducati road model to be produced before the Cagiva takeover

replaced, Tamburini (the 'ta' of Bimota), was the designer responsible for the Paso. When Cagiva, who took over Ducati motorcycle output in 1984, agreed to supply Ducati engines to Bimota in 1985, the situation became even more bizarre; only the Italians could countenance it.

However, their products clearly had a different emphasis, the DB1 being intended solely for sporting use, while the softly-tuned Ducati was aimed at being more of an all-rounder for universal consumption. Certainly, the qualitative improvement in detail fit and finish was something Tamburini brought with him from Bimota, and it indicated that Ducati was looking for a more sophisticated market than had been the case previously. The all-enveloping bodywork/fairing was ingenious in conception and execution, even if the mirrors were hopelessly positioned and offered little protection, as designed, to the rider's hands. For almost the first time on a Ducati, electrics were orderly, sensible and up to the Japanese standard, and the siting of ancillary items, such as the twin oil coolers, in the fairing flanks was original and purposeful, rather than inconvenient and desperate.

While the engine was a straightforward Pantah unit (as described in the DB1 review), it used a single twin-choke Weber carburettor, sited between the cylinders, instead of the traditional brace of Dell'Ortos. As a stop-gap between the latter and the proposed fuel-injection system, it worked tolerably well, but there was a certain amount of splutter and hesitation when the throttle was opened up from 5000 rpm. This hardly prevented the Paso's meagre 74 bhp achieving the bike's 124 mph potential, but it did hinder an otherwise smooth and sophisticated power-plant.

What you would hardly recognize as pedigree Ducati, though, was not the modified 1980 engine, but the total redirection in Italian frame design.

750 F1 was in fact not an exact race replica and was thus overshadowed by the superior DB1 Bimota

Gone was the original Pantah's tubular frame that used the engine as a stressed member, to be replaced by a Japanese-style, square-section, full-cradle design. This, allied to a preload-adjustable Öhlins rear shock and surprisingly progressive 42 mm Marzocchis, gave the Paso a far smoother ride than any Ducati had achieved before, and made nonsense of the hardest-is-best school of Italian suspension design. Steering, on the twin 16 in. wheels, was quick and utterly predictable, while, in the dry at least, the Brembos were irreproachable. The Paso was a joy to ride in all conditions. How many previous Ducatis could you have said that about?

Ducati's 750 F1 Replica up against Suzuki's similar Skoal Bandit replica GSX750R

Ducati Paso

Engine:	Air-cooled 90-degree sohc V-twin	*Front brake:*	Twin 280 mm Brembo discs
Capacity:	748 cc	*Rear brake:*	Single 270 mm disc
Bore × stroke:	88 × 61.5 mm	*Tyres:*	Michelin radials: 130/60V16 front, 160/60V16 rear
Compression ratio:	9.3:1		
Carburation:	Weber 44DCNF twin-barrel	*Wheelbase:*	1450 mm
Power:	74 bhp @ 7900 rpm	*Rake/trail:*	65 degrees/4.1 in.
Torque:	55 ft/lb @ 6350 rpm	*Weight:*	429 lb
Chassis:	Box-section steel double-cradle frame	*Fuel tank:*	4.8 gallons
		Top speed:	120 mph (estimated)
Front suspension:	Marzocchi forks with four-way damping adjustment	*Standard quarter:*	Not available
		Fuel consumption:	55 mpg
Rear suspension:	Öhlins monoshock with infinitely-variable preload	*Range:*	250 miles

Kawasaki GPx750

With such impeccably researched models dominating their litre and $\frac{1}{2}$-litre categories, it was an uncharacteristic lapse of market judgement that led to the ignominious launch of Kawasaki's $\frac{3}{4}$-litre sports bike, the GPz750R, in 1985. Although the bike was identical in appearance to the 900, Kawasaki's belief that it could dominate a class by giving it a Ninja with less of everything bordered on the arrogant, and the bike was hopelessly outclassed by both the Yamaha FZ and the Suzuki GSX750R, which was launched in the same year. It was the last time Kawasaki attempted an assault on any capacity class by adapting another model in their range, and their 1987 750, the GPx, was as new and innovative a motorcycle as either the 600 or 900 had been.

In the hallowed Kawasaki tradition, the GPx was primarily a road bike, targeted at the same market segment dominated by Honda's VF750R, rather than that occupied by the aforementioned sportier

Yamaha and Suzuki. Although unique to that engine capacity, the design borrowed heavily from earlier water-cooled GPzs and manifested Kawasaki's traditional transverse, dohc, 16-valve layout, with the emphasis on less weight, less width and more power. At 200 lb (37 lb lighter than the original GPz750 engine), 16.5 in. across (narrower than an old Triumph twin), and producing 106 bhp (16 bhp up on the lamented 1985 bike), the engine seemed to have realized Kawasaki's goals. The reduction in reciprocating mass by about 60 per cent, combined with lighter, smaller valves, meant higher, safer rpm and extra power. Despite the fact that the GPx seemed most

responsive between 7500 rpm and 10,500 rpm, Kawasaki claimed that only the Yamaha FZ offered more torque in its class. The 150 mph top end was also good enough to match the other three bikes in its category, but until the GPx has been entered for competitive production racing, its exact position in the 750 pecking order is a little difficult to clarify. But as Kawasaki themselves proclaimed, it was the bike's road manners that were of prime importance, and with such a short crank, the engine was not only exceptionally powerful, but also exceptionally smooth.

The chassis, too, was excellent. Carrying 429 lb all-up weight, it had 7 lb less to contain than Honda's VFR, and a good 30 lb in hand over Yamaha's FZ. Surprisingly enough, in an age of rectangular-section-beam aluminium, the GPx had a traditional, black, tubular-steel main frame which, including swinging arm, still managed to tip the scales at less than 29 lb. The main reasons for this dearth of exotica in frame construction were undoubtedly considerations of economy of manufacture and economy of ownership (especially with

the high costs of racing in mind), but the thin-walled, high-tensile steel, which formed an even more old-fashioned double-cradle with top rails running over the engine rather than around it, still managed to control the compact, chunky motor admirably. Complemented at the rear by the established rebound-adjustable, Uni-Trak rising-rate monoshock, and at the front by Kawasaki's new electronically-controlled ESCS compression-damping system, the GPx handled excellently. The retention of a 16 in. front wheel and a 57.5 in. wheelbase (1 in. more than the Suzuki, 1 in. less than the Honda and Yamaha) had as much to do with the GPx's quick-steering sensation as its low overall weight. It literally danced about, but for that reason, judgement was reserved on ultimate handling potential, in case, like the first Suzuki GSX750R, there might have been a slight compromise on stability.

The feeling was that Kawasaki had got the GPx just about right. But would there be a big enough 750 class left in 1987 to support it?

Kawasaki GPx750

Engine:	Water-cooled 16-valve transverse four	Front brake:	Twin dual-piston calipers with 270 mm discs
Capacity:	748 cc	Rear brake:	Single dual-piston caliper with 230 mm disc
Bore × stroke:	68 × 51.5 mm		
Compression ratio:	11.2:1	Tyres:	Dunlop 110/90V16 front, 140/70V18 rear
Carburation:	Four 34 mm CV		
Power:	106 ps @ 10,500 rpm	Wheelbase:	1460 mm (57.5 in.)
Torque:	56.4 ft/lb @ 8000 rpm	Rake/trail:	63 degrees/3.8 in.
Chassis:	Full duplex cradle	Weight:	429 lb
Front suspension:	Telescopic forks with ESCS variable compression damping	Fuel tank:	4.6 gallons
		Top speed:	148 mph (estimated)
		Standard quarter:	11.2 sec (estimated)
Rear suspension:	Uni-Trak monoshock with air-assisted infinitely-variable preload and rebound damping adjustment	Fuel consumption:	Not available
		Range:	185 miles

Honda CB1000F

The rejuvenation of Honda's reputation in the big four-stroke market, initiated by their top-selling VF750R, did not lead, however, to a big-bore development of the bike for the litre class. Rightly or wrongly, Honda saw the key to the domination of the superbike market in 1987 as a simple equation of cost over performance where, for example, the GSX1100's alloy frame or the FZ1000's even more exotically-crafted Deltabox confection might prove unsaleable to a mass audience at a little under £5000. Honda's own sour experience of building a £5250 motorcycle in 1984 (the VF1000R), which subsequently was thrashed by Kawasaki's £2000 cheaper Ninja, may have had something to do with this thinking. However, the general fall-off in world demand for large-capacity motorcycles was probably just as important a factor in influencing their decision not to produce an expensive, alloy-framed VFR1000.

Instead, somewhat coyly, Honda returned to the tried and tested transverse-four prescription eschewed by the company in 1983, but used to devastating effect in their absence by Kawasaki (not to mention Yamaha and Suzuki). The resulting CB1000 was a remarkably traditional, 16-valve, water-cooled, dohc design that seemed, unashamedly, to plagiarize the best features from each of the other manufacturers—overall layout, Kawasaki; alternator behind the crankshaft, Yamaha; pressure-lubricated pistons and rods, Suzuki. With a bore and stroke of 77 × 53.6 mm and a compression ratio of 10.5:1, the new Honda flagship turfed out an impressive and claimed class-beating 132 ps at 9500 rpm, and with maximum torque being delivered only 1000 rpm sooner, this was obviously a very different engine to the tractor-towing grunt legend in the company's earlier V4s.

Similarly, the chassis was a cost-effective affair fashioned from steel and comprising peripheral box-section main rails hugging the engine from both sides, not unlike the FZ1000, but without a full-support cradle underneath. With standard TRAC-activated, twin-pot disc brakes all round, plain understated 41 mm stanchions up front and preload-adjustable Pro-Link monoshock at the rear, the only step into the unknown on the new bike was the adoption of 17 in. rims.

No, what Honda's engineers considered innovative on the CB1000F was neither the engine nor the frame, but rather the all-encompassing bodywork—a sort of giant tupperware fabrication à la Bimota DB1, with every possible protruberance either covered, integrated or sunk into the camouflage. Honda claimed that the styling encouraged a more 'humane, organic feel' to the machine, enabling the rider to develop a far greater sense of intimacy with it. But constant references to the 1000 as the Ford Sierra of motorcycling suggested that Honda may have miscalculated seriously on the bike's overall aesthetics.

In fact, the 1000F, aerodynamic and ergonomically advanced as it undoubtedly was, handled much more like the traditional big Japanese cruisers than either the year-older Suzuki GSX1100 or the Yamaha FZR1000. Not that the bike handled either badly or slowly, but it certainly was not designed as an out-and-out scratching bike; more a dual-purpose sports/tourer with comfort, sophistication and versatility all being of equal importance.

Honda were trying to prove that there were volume sales to be had in the litre-plus category by creating a bike that was not only the fastest but also the most civilized in its capacity. Claims of its 170 mph-plus potential were not verifiable at the end of 1986, but reports of its abundance of smooth, free-revving power gave such claims every probability.

Honda CB1000F

Engine:	Water-cooled 16-valve transverse four
Capacity:	998 cc
Bore × stroke:	77 × 53.6 mm
Compression ratio:	10.5:1
Carburation:	Four 38 mm CV
Power:	132 ps @ 10,000 rpm
Torque:	Not available
Chassis:	Box-section perimeter frame
Front suspension:	41 mm air-assisted Showa forks with anti-dive
Rear suspension:	Pro-Link Showa monoshock with six-way preload and three-way rebound damping adjustment
Front brake:	Twin dual-piston calipers with 296 mm discs
Rear brake:	Single dual-piston caliper with 276 mm disc
Tyres:	Bridgestone Exedra 110/80V17 front, 140/80V17 rear
Wheelbase:	1500 mm
Rake/trail:	62 degrees/Not available
Weight:	509 lb including 1 gallon of fuel
Fuel tank:	4.7 gallons
Top speed:	165 mph
Standard quarter:	11.2 sec @ 124.7 mph
Fuel consumption:	34 mpg
Range:	160 miles

Yamaha FZR1000

With almost as much press clamour for a 1000 cc version of their innovative FZ750 as there had been in 1983 for a full-blown variant of the class-leading 350 two-stroke, Yamaha's FZR1000 was nothing if not inevitable. Conscious, too, that more people might want to buy an FZ750 than the rather unsatisfactory styling allowed, the company sought to weld the world-leading technology of their $\frac{3}{4}$-litre road bike to the bold aesthetics of their world-beating Genesis racer by building an accurate copy for the masses.

The resulting FZR1000, however, was less of an uncompromising sports bike than one might have dared hope for. Although possessing a combination of performance, handling and looks that was uniquely capable of threatening Suzuki's still dominant GSX1100, the FZR was eminently usable in every kind of road situation. After a three-year wait, it seemed that the reign of Kawasaki's GPz900R as the best all-round four-stroke sports bike may have finally been broken.

It would not be too sycophantic to suggest that the Yamaha was pure genius in every respect. Although the engine was no longer the truly innovative component, the chassis was, being derived largely from the works endurance racers and capable of tracing its ancestry back to the first 1982 YZR500 Grand Prix machine campaigned by Kenny Roberts. Fabricated exclusively from cast or beam aluminium, the Deltabox configuration comprised two massive box-section upper rails which ran directly from the steering head to the swing-arm pivot, passing round the cylinder head. A full cradle was achieved by bolting on a smaller, box-section subframe underneath. The rear fork was also in rectangular-section aluminium. Total weight, 26.8 lb.

With incredible strength guaranteed by its construction, and massive torsional resistance achieved through the direct route of the main frame spars, the FZR had no need of infinitely-variable,

complicated suspension. Front forks were rugged, but simple, 41 mm units, adjustable only for preload and devoid of any anti-dive arrangement. The rear suspension was the Grand Prix-developed monocross rising-rate system, positioned as low as possible beneath the bike's centre-of-mass line. Brakes were colossal 320 mm drilled discs, activated by twin opposed-piston calipers, and the wheels were 17 in. and 18 in. items shod with ultra-low-profile radial tyres.

The litre mill was basically a bore-and-stroke job on the original FZ750, increasing dimensions from the latter's 68 × 51.6 mm to 75 × 56 mm. Despite the increase in capacity, Yamaha managed to keep

the 1000's block to the same size as the smaller bike's. They installed bigger carburettors (37 mm instead of 34 mm), bigger inlet valves (23.5 mm instead of 21 mm) and bigger exhaust valves (25 mm instead of 23 mm) to feed the larger chambers. Initial problems with vibration led to a great deal of work on the rod/piston/crankshaft assembly, resulting in components that were actually lighter than the smaller bike's. These were cooled, à la GSX, by under-piston oil jets as an addition to the FZR's original liquid-cooling system. Like the 750, the engine was canted 45 degrees forward in the frame for optimum handling.

Yamaha FZR1000

Engine:	Liquid-cooled dohc 20-valve four-stroke four
Capacity:	989 cc
Bore × stroke:	75 × 56 mm
Compression ratio:	11.2:1
Carburation:	Four 37 mm Mikuni
Power:	125 ps @ 10,000 rpm
Torque:	76 ft/lb @ 8500 rpm
Chassis:	Aluminium Deltabox full-cradle perimeter frame
Front suspension:	41 mm fork with preload adjustment
Rear suspension:	Monocross monoshock with variable preload
Front brake:	Twin dual-opposed-piston calipers with floating 320 mm discs
Rear brake:	Single opposed-piston caliper with solid 267 mm disc
Tyres:	Pirelli radials: 120/70V17 front, 160/60V18 rear
Wheelbase:	1470 mm
Rake/trail:	65 degrees/3.7 in.
Weight:	448 lb (dry)
Fuel tank:	5.6 gallons
Top speed:	165 mph (estimated)
Standard quarter:	11.0 sec
Fuel consumption:	36 mpg (estimated)
Range:	Not available

The power was both abundant and uncannily smooth. Even before official speed tests, with over 125 bhp on tap, the FZR proved that its target of 170 mph seemed readily attainable. It progressed beautifully from 2000 to 11,000 rpm with hardly a noticeable step. Handling, too, was irreproachable, exhibiting fantastically quick steering for such a large-capacity bike and astounding stability. As 1987 dawned, the FZR represented the state of the art in motorcycle chassis and engine design. It was the most eloquent statement yet of how far motorcycle design had come.

Yamaha TZR250

The special significance of the 250 cc class in the Japanese domestic home market provided a constant incentive for the factories to come up with ever-faster and better-handling machinery in the $\frac{1}{4}$-litre bracket. First the Honda four-stroke VT250 and then the Suzuki RG250 Gamma two-stroke made it to these shores as a direct result of the favourable reception they had received in Japan. Of course, not all the 250s available in the country of origin made it to export, but when Yamaha tested the water by providing a TZR250 to race-journalist Mat Oxley to campaign in the 1986 Isle of Man TT

production class and were rewarded with the first 100 mph 250 TT lap, suddenly the writing seemed to be on the wall for the Suzuki RG250 Gamma.

In fact, though owing little to the pioneering RD250/350LC series that dominated the stroker market in the early 1980s, the TZR too was a water-cooled parallel twin of the traditional Yamaha recipe. A bore and stroke of 56.4 × 50 mm shared

with the latest TZ series racers, combined with identical crankcase-induction and the familiar YPVS variable exhaust-port system, established the TZR250 as the first genuine 200 bhp per litre 250. Together with a posilube gearbox and pukka expansion pipes running from the exhaust ports, the TZR came so near the mechanical specification of Yamaha's world-championship-winning TZ250 that there was little cause to doubt the factory's claimed power output.

The bike's outstanding feature, however, was not its engine but its chassis, modelled in the new Yamaha corporate Deltabox style, comprising a massive twin aluminium beam running from headstock to swinging arm and precious little else. This fabrication, 40 per cent lighter and 30 per cent stronger than steel, dwarfed the engine to the point of aesthetic absurdity when the race-replica bodywork was removed.

Complemented at the rear by the TZ-type rising-rate De Carbon monoshock controlling the massive aluminium swing arm, and at the front by huge 39 mm variable compression-damping telescopic forks, the TZR managed to keep its weight to a modest 280 lb, just bettering the standard established by the hitherto class-dominating RG250 Gamma, but of course with a significant power advantage to spare over the latter. Even the wheels were hollow three-spoke race replicas and the single four-pot disc brakes, front and rear, followed established Yamaha racing practice.

Little surprise, then, that the bike was a gem, able to dive in late, to change course, to process the most erroneous and erratic of rider inputs almost unflustered. To speak of 'response' was inappropriate—unless you had ridden one, you couldn't imagine what the tester might have been talking about. It was tiny, light, unbelievably stable and very, very powerful. Though the YPVS system gave the bike some semblance of mid-range power, delivery was only marginally more flexible than the all-or-nothing-at-all Gamma, with the real jerk of torque commencing at 7000 rpm, and culminating at 9000 before everything tailed off abruptly after five figures. And with the factory offering a 25 per cent extra-power race kit (though for a cool £2000), the TZR's domination of the tracks looked assured for some time.

Would the depressed British market of 1987 stand the TZR250? With 20,000 units sold in Japan alone, Yamaha was willing to take that gamble.

Yamaha TZR250

Engine:	Liquid-cooled parallel twin with case-reed induction
Capacity:	249 cc
Bore × stroke:	56.4 × 50 mm
Compression ratio:	5.9:1
Carburation:	Two 28 mm flat-slide Mikuni
Power:	50 ps @ 10,000 rpm
Torque:	27 ft/lb @ 9750 rpm
Chassis:	Aluminium Deltabox frame with engine as stressed member
Front suspension:	39 mm fork with preload and damping adjustment
Rear suspension:	Monocross monoshock with variable preload
Front brake:	Single dual-opposed-piston caliper with 320 mm floating disc
Rear brake:	Single opposed-piston caliper with 210 mm solid disc
Tyres:	100/80H17 front, 120/80H18 rear (tubeless)
Wheelbase:	1375 mm
Rake/trail:	64 degrees/3.7 in.
Weight:	281 lb (dry)
Fuel tank:	3.5 gallons
Top speed:	125 mph (estimated)
Standard quarter:	Not available
Fuel consumption:	Not available
Range:	140 miles (estimated)

Osprey Collector's Library Backlist

AJS and Matchless – The Postwar Models
Roy Bacon
0 85045 536 7

Ariel – The Postwar Models
Roy Bacon
0 85045 537 5

BMW Twins & Singles
Roy Bacon
0 85045 699 1

British Motorcycles of the 1930s
Roy Bacon
0 85045 657 6

BSA Gold Star and Other Singles
Roy Bacon
0 85045 447 6

BSA Twins & Triples
Roy Bacon
0 85045 368 2

Classic British Scramblers
Don Morley
0 85045 649 5

Classic British Trials Bikes
Don Morley
0 85045 545 6

Classic British Two-Stroke Trials Bikes
Don Morley
0 85045 745 9

Classic Motorcycle Racer Tests
Alan Cathcart
0 85045 589 8

Ducati Singles
Mick Walker
0 85045 605 3

Ducati Twins
Mick Walker
0 85045 634 7

Gilera Road Racers
Raymond Ainscoe
0 85045 675 4

Honda—The Early Classic Motorcycles
Roy Bacon
0 85045 596 0

Kawasaki – Sunrise to Z1
Roy Bacon
0 85045 544 8

Military Motorcycles of World War 2
Roy Bacon
0 85045 618 5

Moto Guzzi Singles
Mick Walker
0 85045 712 2

Moto Guzzi Twins
Mick Walker
0 85045 650 9

MV Agusta
Mick Walker
0 85045 711 4

Norton Singles
Roy Bacon
0 85045 485 9

Norton Twins
Roy Bacon
0 85045 423 9

Royal Enfield – The Postwar Models
Roy Bacon
0 85045 459 X

Spanish Post-war Road and Racing Motorcycles
Mick Walker
0 85045 705 X

Spanish Trials Bikes
Don Morley
0 85045 663 0

Suzuki Two-Strokes
Roy Bacon
0 85045 588 X

Triumph Twins & Triples
Roy Bacon
0 85045 700 9

Velocette Flat Twins
Roy Bacon
0 85045 632 0

Villiers Singles & Twins
Roy Bacon
0 85045 486 7

Vincent Vee Twins
Roy Harper
0 85045 435 2

Yamaha Dirtbikes
Colin MacKellar
0 85045 660 6

Yamaha Two-Stroke Twins
Colin MacKellar
0 85045 582 0

Write for a free catalogue of motorcycle books to
The Sales Manager,
Osprey Publishing Limited,
27A Floral Street,
London WC2E 9DP